THE STIRLING PRIZE

DEDICATED TO GILES WORSLEY
ARCHITECTURE CRITIC
1961–2006

First published 2006 by Merrell Publishers Limited

HEAD OFFICE
81 Southwark Street
London SE1 0HX

NEW YORK OFFICE
49 West 24th Street, 8th Floor
New York, NY 10010

www.merrellpublishers.com

in association with

RIBA TRUST
66 Portland Place
London W1B 1AD

www.riba.org

Publisher Hugh Merrell
Editorial Director Julian Honer
US Director Joan Brookbank
Sales and Marketing Manager Kim Cope
Sales and Marketing Executive Sarah Unitt
Sales and Marketing Assistant Abigail Coombs
US Sales and Marketing Assistant Elizabeth Choi
Managing Editor Anthea Snow
Project Editors Claire Chandler, Rosanna Fairhead
Junior Editor Helen Miles
Art Director Nicola Bailey
Designer Paul Shinn
Production Manager Michelle Draycott
Production Controller Sadie Butler

British Library Cataloguing-in-Publication Data:
Chapman, Tony
The Stirling Prize : ten years of architecture and innovation
1.Architecture – Awards – Great Britain 2.Architecture –
Great Britain 3.Architecture, Modern – 20th century
4.Architecture, Modern – 21st century
I.Title
720.7'941

ISBN 1 85894 321 3

Designed by Claudia Schenk
Picture research by Caz Facey
Edited by Tom Neville
Indexed by Christine Shuttleworth
Printed and bound in Slovenia

Jacket, front
Gateshead Millennium Bridge, Tyne and Wear, by Wilkinson Eyre
Architects (see pp. 146–49); photograph by Graeme Peacock

Jacket, back
1996: The Centenary Building, University of Salford, Manchester,
by Hodder Associates (see pp. 20–23)
1997: The Music School, Stuttgart, Germany, by Michael Wilford
and Partners (see pp. 38–41)
1998: American Air Museum in Britain, Imperial War Museum,
Duxford, Cambridge, by Foster and Partners (see pp. 56–59)
1999: NatWest Media Centre, Lord's Cricket Ground, London
NW8, by Future Systems (see pp. 84–87)
2000: Peckham Library and Media Centre, London SE15,
by Alsop & Störmer (see pp. 106–109)
2001: Magna Science Adventure Centre, Rotherham, South
Yorkshire, by Wilkinson Eyre Architects (see pp. 126–29)
2003: Laban, London SE8, by Herzog & de Meuron (see
pp. 166–69)
2004: 30 St Mary Axe, London EC3, by Foster and Partners
(see pp. 184–87)
2005: The Scottish Parliament, Edinburgh, by EMBT/RMJM
(see pp. 202–205)

THE STIRLING PRIZE

TEN YEARS OF ARCHITECTURE AND INNOVATION

.TONY CHAPMAN

MERRELL
LONDON · NEW YORK

RIBA ⚏ Trust

CONTENTS

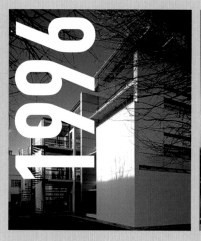
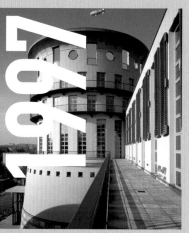

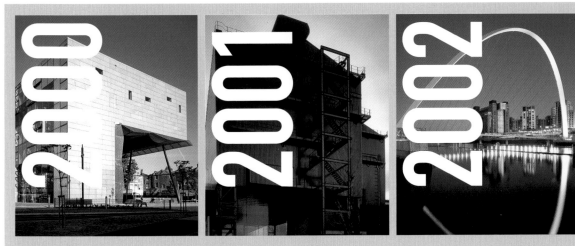

THE STIRLING PRIZE FOR ARCHITECTURE
RIBA/THE SUNDAY TIMES BUILDING OF THE YEAR

1996 THE CENTENARY BUILDING/HODDER ASSOCIATES

1997 THE STUTTGART MUSIC SCHOOL/
SIR JAMES STIRLING & MICHAEL WILFORD AND PARTNERS

1998 THE AMERICAN AIR MUSEUM IN BRITAIN/
FOSTER AND PARTNERS

THE MAKING OF THE STIRLING PRIZE

STIRLING: THE DUCT-TAPE YEARS

It's not easy to remember what architecture was like back then. It may have been only ten years ago, but in 1996 we were still in the architectural Dark Ages. A decade earlier, then RIBA president Michael Manser (still reeling from Prince Charles's onslaught on architects launched at what was meant to be a celebration of the one-hundred-and-fiftieth anniversary of the RIBA and the award of the Royal Gold Medal to Charles Correa) wrote in his introduction to the *40 Under Forty* exhibition of young talent: "This generation of architects is a slightly lost generation. The opportunities for new buildings have been smaller in their time for two reasons – the circumstances of the economy and obsessive conservation. ... Architects of this generation have not had much chance to make three-dimensional architecture."

That sad state of affairs was little changed when the RIBA's Awards Group met in 1994 to discuss how to improve its system. If anything, the economy had worsened. The Awards Group had been struggling to make ends meet with the help of the ghost of Marley plc, a shrinking trust fund established in 1988 thanks to a £100,000 endowment by the tile manufacturer. On the table was a proposal to "build a single-focused PR campaign around the event, to amalgamate all awards ceremonies into one major event at the Albert Hall or similar" (is there anything similar?) and "to sell tables for dinner, to use a high-profile presenter and make a profit for the RIBA". One irate member responded: "Rather than a celebration of the best in British architecture and an excellent opportunity for communicating good design to a wider public, it now appears that the awards are being turned into some sort of financial milch cow."

In those bad old days, much of the best work of our major architects was being done abroad. Fifteen years of Conservative government had created a conservative society (we had a Department of National Heritage, not one of Culture), and most clients were cautious in their tastes and therefore in their commissioning. And most of the public were equally conservative, or so it was assumed. So in February 1995 Marco Goldschmied, yet to be RIBA president, proposed that buildings designed in Europe by RIBA members should be considered for awards. The group agreed that judging from photographs alone was unsatisfactory and that generous sponsorship would be needed if its members were to be going on lots of European jollies. It was almost three years before Goldschmied had his way, and even then the EU judging went ahead without sponsorship.

But by then everything had changed anyway. Mr Blair and his handmaiden Cool Britannia had arrived. The economy was on the up. And as luck and the electorate would have it, one of the greatest instruments of change was a Conservative legacy: the Lottery. In a few years it was to bring work for architects at all levels, from high-profile arts projects (many funded by the Arts Lottery Fund headed by RIBA president David Rock) to small church halls and scout huts (one of which won an award in 1998). Architecture was no longer a dirty word. It was even, of itself, cool. Instead of mumbling something apologetic when asked what they

Instead of mumbling something apologetic when asked what they did, architects found themselves the main attraction at dinner parties.

ABOVE Stephen Hodder, the 1996 Stirling Prize winner and Young Architect of the Year, is interviewed by the author outside his Centenary Building at the University of Salford.

did, architects found themselves the main attraction at dinner parties. Prince Charles and his views were marginalized. The Modernists were back. And one of the main reasons for all of this was the Stirling Prize.

The Building of the Year had been going since 1993, the personal choice of the RIBA president from a handful of national awards. The search was on for a sponsor to put the awards on a more professional footing. Ever an optimist, Chris Palmer, the RIBA's director of communications at the time, reported that he needed between £60,000 and £70,000 in order to offer a prize of £20,000 and put the awards on a par with the Booker Prize for fiction. Approaches were made to a number of potential sponsors, including Birse Construction, which, perhaps unsurprisingly, could not see that there was enough in it for the company. Finally, in September 1995, a three-year sponsorship deal was done with *The Sunday Times*. The awards were to be known as the RIBA/Sunday Times Architecture Awards, or vice versa, with £20,000 specifically provided as prize money for the Building of the Year. "The link poses no threat to the autonomy of the awards", wrote Nancy Mills, a clearly defensive awards administrator.

Over dinner ten years on, in a Marylebone High Street restaurant, Hugh Pearman, the architecture critic of *The Sunday Times*; Jane Priestman, chair of the Awards Group in 1996, the RIBA's awards governing body; Chris Palmer and I (I have run the awards since Palmer left in 1998) reminisced:

CP We did something about 1993 which was the President's Choice. I started calling it the Building of the Year because the President's Choice sounded like a poor claret. And I think previously, about '88, the RIBA had been feeling left out and on the back of Hugh's idea started what was in effect a Building of the Year.

HP That's how I remember it. And so we had the notion that we'd have a building of the year. I mean, one could only have so much of Lord St John of Fawsley. He was charming, delightful and funny, and for about a week every year that was fine, but we were paying money just for the running costs of that award [the Royal Fine Art Commission Award]. My editor had changed. It had been very much an Andrew Neil thing; he and Norman were chums from the *Economist* days. So my memory is that I think I rang you and said, can we join forces?

CP So we met in the restaurant on the corner – we're sitting in the wrong restaurant!

HP Yes, Marylebone High Street it was.

CP What is now La Famiglia Getti.

HP And you said, but why don't you express this £20k as the prize? That was the bones of it.

CP The reason I thought that was because the year before, when I first mooted the idea, I remember Richard MacCormac being really pleased for Nicholas Grimshaw when he won with Waterloo, and I actually thought it shouldn't be a prize that people are pleased for other people to win. And no disrespect to Richard, but if there was twenty grand in there he wouldn't be really pleased.

ABOVE The Stirling judges' trip to Stuttgart in 1997 to see Michael Wilford's realization of James Stirling's masterplan was their first outside the United Kingdom, but the people disagreed with their choice of the Music School as winner. In the bottom two images, Chris Palmer and Nancy Mills count the People's Choice award, won by Mark Guard.

Concern was also expressed in the Awards Group about such a major prize being given at the behest, the whim even, of one person, albeit the president of the RIBA. Instead, the prize would be judged by the president, Hugh Pearman of *The Sunday Times* and a prominent lay person nominated by the RIBA.

The Building of the Year was dead; long live the Stirling Prize for the Building of the Year. All that remained was to come up with a name for it and tell the world the glad tidings.

HP I got very worried that the prize had to have a name: should it be the Sunday Times/RIBA Building of the Year, the RIBA/Sunday Times ... all that kind of thing. And I have here a letter to my editor, my note to you, Chris, in September 1995, tying up the loose ends: "We need to have an award that is triply effective, combining the thoroughness and large entry for the existing RIBA Awards scheme with the cachet of the existing Sunday Times RFAC Award."

TC Your style's improved, Hugh.

HP "Plus adding for the first time the £20k prize for the Building of Year, which will make the prize unique and we all hope close to the Booker Prize for architecture that we first envisaged when we conceived the Sunday Times Award eight years ago." Sorry about the language. But then later I thought, no, we shouldn't be thinking about the Booker, we should be thinking about the Turner. And that was 1995, the best ever, Brian Eno giving the prize to Damien Hirst for his *Mother and Child, Divided*, the cow and calf cut in half. I remember watching the Turner Prize and thinking, we want something like that – we need a name that has a resonance. That's when I thought of Stirling, because like Turner it means something, while Booker was just a food distributor. So I rang you up, saying, Stirling Prize, so that gave it a name. I remember ringing Jane and she said something like, wow, yes.

JP Yes, I'm not into lengthy conversations on the phone.

HP   But would the family wear it? So the person delegated to put it to the Stirling family was me. And Mary said, Jim never had much time for the RIBA because he never thought they put much work his way.

CP Probably typical of the nation's architects.

HP So she ummed and ahhed for a little while. And she consulted Michael Wilford about it, and Michael said, yes, I think it's a great idea. But Mary's view was that if only there had been such an award as this when Jim was young which would somehow encourage the new people coming along. Mary's take on it was that if new talent could be recognized by this award then Jim would have approved. So in later years I felt slightly uncomfortable when the likes of Foster won it. ... On the other hand, you can't say certain people are excluded because they are too good or too old or too rich.

TC There was a lovely half-reported piece in the minutes about Mary being asked if she was content for Jim's name to be used in perpetuity of course – and she said, yes, she was. Then she went on to ask, how would my newly founded foundation benefit?

ABOVE The prize came of age in 1998: (from top) there was a major exhibition at the RIBA; Norman Foster was announced as winner by Peter Mandelson; Roland Paoletti was the first RIBA Client of the Year; and everyone played Jenga after dinner.

OPPOSITE The 1999 Stirling judges – Rick Mather, Amanda Baillieu, Stella McCartney, Michael Manser and Marco Goldschmied – visited (from top) Sto in Germany, Ranelagh School in Dublin, and ended up at the NatWest Media Centre at Lord's, which, after heated debate, they finally declared the winner.

JP I remember that. I replied in the negative, except in terms of kudos.

TC Except it might have been put the other way round: could your foundation support the prize as we can't necessarily rely on commercial sponsors, as we found out? One of the debates was, should we set something up on the basis of commercial sponsorship and not endowment? Marco was concerned about that.

HP Rightly, I think.

JP I'd just come in as chairman of the Awards Committee. And I said, go for it. And you said, for one year, and I said, under no circumstances, it would have to be a minimum of three, and sure enough [*The Sunday Times*] pulled out [before] the third year.

HP Yes we did, and I was very upset about that because I was expecting it to continue. But the third year hit a moment when there was an economy drive and it was an easy thing to trim off because it didn't come out of editorial budgets.

CP Hugh Pearman dumped me by email, probably the first person in the history of this new medium to dump someone by email.

HP But we had signed you up by fax.

JP Had you pulled out after one year, Stirling wouldn't exist now.

HP No, but even so it left you in enough trouble.

TC Fortunately we had a tame journal we could call on. [The *RIBA Journal* sponsored the prize between 1998 and 2000.]

HP Exactly, and in the long run it was better because to be associated with one paper means other media are always going to be jealous.

TC Particularly as it was Murdoch.

HP A) It was Murdoch, B) *The Sunday Times*, C) it was me. Reading my notes here, proposing the Stirling Prize, the name was separate from any sponsor there might happen to be. I said it didn't even have to be the RIBA; it could be someone else doing the prize.

TC Marco was particularly interested in widening the awards to be European; in fact, he wanted them to be worldwide. He reckoned British Airways might stump up the £15,000 it would cost to fly judges round the world. And then you were pragmatic, Chris, it says in these minutes. You proposed limiting them to Europe.

HP So it must have been the second year of the prize when I spent a lot of time going to see another one that should have won, Will Alsop's Grand Bleu in Marseilles.

TC Another one that got away.

CP But that first year – we shouldn't be embarrassed about non-iconic buildings winning because I think Stephen Hodder winning was very good for the architecture profession, certainly for a lot of young architects coming out of the recession. People thought it wasn't going to be the annual Norman Foster Award; there is hope for us all in that.

HP There is that, because if it had been launched two years before it would have been Nicholas Grimshaw, Michael Hopkins ...

In February 1997 the Awards Group agreed that the first Stirling Party had been a success, although the slide presentation should have been slicker and "there was unanimous agreement that the present in-house catering arrangements were wholly unacceptable at such a prestigious occasion which was attended by many important clients". It was agreed to invite Neil Kinnock to present the second Stirling Prize, but the electorate had other ideas. No need now to go for a man who had twice failed to become PM. Instead of going with losers, we could go for a winner: what better way to jump on the Cool Britannia bandwagon than to invite its driver, Prime Minister Blair, to present the prize, or if he couldn't make it (he couldn't), his arts minister, Chris Smith?

Everything was becoming more ambitious in year two. There was to be a video, commissioned from me, to accompany the exhibition, with the shortlisted architects invited to chose a piece of music that fitted their building, a bit like *Desert Island Discs*. Richard Rogers chose Pink Floyd's 'Another Brick in the Wall' to go with his Thames Valley University Learning Resource Centre in Slough. More obscurely, Will Alsop picked Gavin Bryars's 'Titanic Hymn (Autumn)' from *The Sinking of the Titanic* to accompany his Grand Bleu in Marseilles, perhaps a premonition that, despite being hot favourite with William Hill at 6–4, a dark horse in the shape of Michael Wilford (4–1) was coming up on the rails? The RIBA was at it, too: swept along by 1997 election fever, it was decided that the exhibition would also include a 'People's Choice'. The winner was Mark Guard's roof-top apartment in Paris, with 35 per cent of the popular vote.

HP We were talking about the time before emails; it was before PowerPoint as well. It was the third year when Marco Goldschmied leaned casually on the podium, a duct-tape podium, in the Florence Hall, putting his elbow on the forward button of the slide carousel, and we saw all the winners flashing before our eyes. But that was also the Jenga year, which my senior editor on *The Sunday Times*, David Mills, remembers with enormous fondness.

CP For some reason it was very delayed, and it taught me the single most important thing about parties is just to get everyone absolutely plastered.

Of which more later …

THE VIDEOTAPE YEARS: ARCHITECTURE ON TELEVISION

I'm not sure where the idea that architecture and television don't go together comes from, but it was accepted as a truism for much of the 1970s, 1980s and early 1990s, coinciding with my own TV career. It took a Royal Commission to get buildings on the box and then it was largely knocking copy. My own attempts were generally turned down, although a few slipped under the net, usually heavily disguised as something else: Paris and London lifestyles (actually the *Grands Projets* and the lack of London equivalents), 'Village Fate' (ex-urbanism) and, most notably and honestly, 'The Max Factor', the Modernists' riposte to the Prince of Wales, which helped launch the media career of Maxwell Hutchinson, then president of the RIBA.

ABOVE The first televised year was 2000. Channel 4 cameras followed judges Tracey Emin, Michael Manser, Amanda Levete, Eric Parry and Amanda Baillieu on a trip that took in (from top) the London Eye, Sainsbury's in Greenwich and the New Art Gallery Walsall.

Others were using still more subtle approaches. *The Late Show* did a lot for architecture. The late-night BBC2 slot was the first to cover architecture as one of the arts on television. Then there was *Building Sites*, the first programme really to explore buildings. It did it very briefly, but you can cover a lot of building in three or four minutes. Norman Foster chose the jumbo jet, which made a cracking programme, and Jan Kaplicky picked the Humber Bridge, with Diane Keaton doing Frank Lloyd Wright's Ennis House. But more often than not, what the camera was up to was more interesting than what the celebrity presenter had to say. Others went down the heritage route (still a popular one): the older the building – and often the presenter, too – the better. Clearly there was an audience for architecture, provided you said it was about buildings and didn't mention the 'A' word.

It wasn't such a preposterous proposition after all: that people might be interested in the things in which they spend most of their lives, even that they might have intelligent things to say about what they want from the buildings in which they work, rest and play. But the general perception among the public – and all too many architects – back then was that clients should be seen and not heard. The idea that clients could be there to do anything more than sign the cheques and live with the consequences, that architects and clients could form an intelligent partnership, that *Grand Designs* could provide one of the most popular hours in a week's television; such ideas belonged to an idealized future.

Now that the formula has been so overworked, it is almost equally hard to acknowledge that *Changing Rooms* was a kind of breakthrough in that it credited people with an interest in design (if not necessarily with taste). It did for a new generation what Habitat had done in the 1960s and 1970s and what IKEA was doing in the 1990s: it made design attractive and attainable. It was a flat-pack component of Cool Britannia, a self-assembly bookend, the other end of which was the Stirling Prize. In the middle came (and remains) *Grand Designs*, which made the other important connection – that between property and architecture. Until that time, property programmes had referred vaguely to designers, those people who wear wacky coloured shirts hanging over their trousers and shout a lot. *Grand Designs* was the first to acknowledge that good buildings actually need architects, and yes, they may be a bit dull in their black suits, but if you can get them to talk English they do have some rather good things to say.

Marco Goldschmied knew the value of publicity. He had been trying to get the Building of the Year on television since 1995. In the pre-digital era, however, television was a buyer's market. I knew from bitter experience that it was hard as hell to sell an idea to a programme commissioner (or I might still be making those architecture programmes rather than writing this book). There was clearly a gap in the TV awards market. Books had their Bookers, television its Baftas, film its Oscars and art its Turner. Each of these art forms had signed its personalized pact with the Devil, although at least two of them, television and film, clearly had home fixtures. Books and art were quickly made aware that for them there had to be a trade-off: publicity in exchange for controversy. Was the RIBA prepared to do the same? Members and staff were both divided on the issue. Many architects (though not all)

Clearly there was an audience for architecture, provided you said it was about buildings and didn't mention the 'A' word.

ABOVE Boys' toys: the 2002 winner, the Gateshead Millennium Bridge, was raised by RIBA president Paul Hyett, assisted by Kate Mosse, Farshid Moussavi, Wayne Hemingway and Paul Finch.

preferred the safe, low-key *status quo*; others, including the PR wing of the RIBA, simply wanted to know where to sign. The BBC still ummed and ahhed. Chris Palmer reported to the Awards Group in April 1996 that the BBC *Late Show* was interested in covering the presentation of the prize and that Channel 4 had also shown interest.

As the RIBA's head of press at that time, I put together a pitch to try to sell Stirling to the broadcasters. It went like this:

- The Stirling Prize is architecture's top prize.
- It is awarded for buildings that work, not for ones that are merely pretty.
- Architecture is fashionable; even the government seems to have decided it's 'cool'. There are more column inches in newspapers and magazines devoted to it than ever before. Only television lags behind, preferring to deal with heritage and housing (although of course these are two significant categories in the shortlist for the Stirling Prize).
- Architecture is controversial. Yes, the Prince of Wales started the debate. That battle may be over, but it awoke passions in the public over the way their immediate environment looks, and those passions are still very much alive.
- Architects are every bit as good at bitching and bickering as their literary counterparts. Controversy over the shortlist within the profession is just as great as that concerning the Booker shortlist. It's just that at present it's not rehearsed in public so much. It could be.
- Buildings are much more televisual than books or paintings, both of which make perfectly good TV awards. This is because:
    - you can walk around them;
    - you can talk to people who use them (all the buildings have to be complete and most are in use);
    - you don't need actors to bring them to life.
- Architecture is less elitist than these other forms precisely because it is not just an art form; it is a practical art. We couldn't live without the work of architects, hence its intrinsic appeal.
- The judging process is more transparent and interesting. We can follow the judges – including non-architect judges – as they visit buildings all around the European Union.

As well as pitching to the BBC, I even courted ITV, somewhat optimistically, I admit, in the shape of Carlton's managing director, Colin Stanbridge, with whom I used to work on *Nationwide*. The old-boy network failed to come up trumps.

In September 1997 Chris Palmer was still awaiting the outcome of negotiations that were underway with the BBC. The corporation's commitment, he said cryptically, "would considerably affect sponsorship opportunities". Alan Yentob, that rarity, a cultured TV executive, was keen but could not persuade his philistine colleagues. Channel 4 already had the Turner, and the BBC had its Designer of the

Architects are every bit as good at bitching and bickering as their literary counterparts. Controversy over the shortlist within the profession is just as great as that concerning the Booker shortlist.

Year. Even Sky had signed up the Royal Fine Art Commission and appropriated our moniker, The Building of the Year. The prize's inventors reckoned it would take between two years (Chris Palmer) and five years (Hugh Pearman) to get on television: it actually took four.

It was Marco Goldschmied, as RIBA president, who brokered the successful deal and who must take the credit for finally moving architecture into the late twentieth century. He told me:

Apart from the sustainability agenda, the thing I was hoping to do was to raise the profile of architecture and by implication that of the RIBA. It seemed to me that television was the way. The RIBA had made various attempts but always on its own terms and always to BBC2, which was seen as the culture channel, so it had a rather old-fashioned approach: we do it on Thursday and would you like to bring your cameras along and televise the event? And the answer, not surprisingly, was no, because it was rotten TV. I think the breakthrough was with Stephen Phillips [our media adviser and a former Channel 4 arts correspondent] reformulating it and saying, let's go to somebody more cutting edge, as Channel 4 was certainly at the time, and say, if you did it, what format would you want? So it all came about because we were prepared to give the television people *carte blanche* to say what they wanted. Even the first one got over a million viewers. I don't know how many the Booker and Turner get, but it's probably more than those two combined. And I think it also caught the wave, with design becoming important and even housebuilders starting to use more high-profile designers and realizing that design actually sells. I think there was a bandwagon effect, and I suspect that televising Stirling gave some kind of push to that bandwagon.

So Stephen Phillips, Roula Konzotis, the RIBA's director of communications, and myself went to see Channel 4 and we hammered out the format. They only agreed to do it on a one-off basis, but we were delighted to come away from Channel 4 headquarters with a deal. There were still things to do with copyright and architects' consent, but the decision in principle was achieved on the spot. There is a school of thought that says it has changed the nature of the prize; it has changed over a number of years in a number of ways. You couldn't enter a building if it hadn't been up for three years, and now you can't enter if it's been up for more than two, so it's moved away from the solid virtues of architecture as something that has to have a test of integrity and durability. The other thing that has changed is that we have so much media coverage these days, not only in the journals but also in the national press and TV and websites, so that the building you did in 2002 is old hat. We consume new buildings at a completely different rate than we did in the 1960s and '70s. It's part of the way society has evolved, and the Stirling has just moved with the times.

Channel 4 chose the production company ZCZ, which was owned by Waldemar Januszczak. Since he was a former commissioning arts editor at Channel 4, it was

ABOVE The 2003 judges – Chris Wilkinson, Justine Frischmann, Isabel Allen, Julian Barnes and George Ferguson – visited (from top) BedZED, the Great Court at the British Museum, and Plymouth Theatre Royal, where they re-enacted the Beatles' album cover for *Help!* But there was only ever going to be one winner: Laban.

the obvious way to go for presenter and production company. The plan was to go live, but as the weeks towards transmission raced by, the channel got cold feet and went for 'as-live' instead.

HP I remember the first year it was televised. There was all that hanging around while TV got its act together. I was sitting with Mary Stirling and we looked at each other and I said, Mary, have we created a Frankenstein's monster? But she remained supportive. Her daughters and sons still turn up. But it was redeemed by Will's wonderful speech.

TC Which couldn't have happened if there hadn't been the time delays because he wouldn't have been as pissed.

HP Yes, there should be more of that.

One thing television could and indubitably did do was to up the status of the prize. We'd got nowhere the first time we'd invited Tony Blair, unsurprisingly. In 2000 we tried again and were able to dangle a carrot in the shape of television. In the end he couldn't make it, but he did offer to do a video. Goldschmied was all for turning him down. If he can't be bothered to show up – who does he think he is? But we graciously accepted the gracious offer. This is what Blair said to Januszczak, and it shows how far government attitudes to architecture had changed:

There was a time when people thought that all modern architecture was rubbish and basically the only building that was good was the one you saw in history books. Now, we should be really proud of our heritage – it's fantastic – but what's happening now is that we're getting great new buildings and designs and those are happening not just in some of the public buildings but also businesses and industry. If they are opening new headquarters or developing a new factory they are looking at the design, so the issue of design is far more important now than it was even ten years ago. And so it is important both in business and in government to be treating this far more seriously. It can [make] a real difference [to] the way that people work and live. Good design is not just good for people who work in buildings that are well designed or live in houses that are well designed; it is also good in terms of crime, safety and the environment. I think there's a whole different type of agenda around architecture and design in public policy terms that would have been considered eccentric five or six years ago.

This went down a storm at the Stirling presentation in the Wellcome Wing of the Science Museum in London. The same cannot be said for the ZCZ-induced delays in the announcement, which the company insisted on blaming on the judges' inability to reach a decision. In fact, they were locked away, getting quietly drunk and dying to be allowed to come down to join everyone else for the dinner that no one was allowed to eat until ZCZ had sorted out the links, both Januszczak's and those to the outside-broadcast truck. And no one was taking better advantage of the two-hour delay than Will Alsop. Win or lose, it was all going to be a bit of a haze for him, as the

ABOVE In 2004 the toughest jury ever turned out to be the only unanimous one – so far: (from top) Antony Gormley, Deborah Bull, Ted Cullinan, Isabel Allen and Francine Houben at the Spire, Dublin, with Kevin McCloud; in the Kunsthaus, Graz; in Coventry; and at the top of the 'Gherkin'.

audience and Kensington and Chelsea planners, who were on the wrong end
of his alcohol-fuelled wrath, knew only too well. Only the TV audience was left in
ignorance, as Channel 4 bleeped his expletive (it could just as easily have cut it).

We had stepped into the brave new world of television, and there was no going
back. As Goldschmied puts it:

It has become a very slick production and lost some of its nitty-gritty
professional integrity. But perhaps we architects are too close to it, we want
to keep control of it – that goes with the territory – but it's in the public realm
now. I think there is a danger that it becomes populist to the extent that the
jurors could become influenced by what is popular. So the upside is that
architecture has benefited; the downside is that we have moved out of the
slightly cosy professional world into the wider world.

Which is where the clients live, after all, and where architecture has to be.

ABOVE Piers Gough, one of the
2005 judges, relaxes in the
Fawood yurt (top), while Max
Fordham checks out the Jubilee
Library's services, and Jack
Pringle, Joan Bakewell and
Gough view the art in the Lewis
Glucksman Gallery in Cork.

.JUDGES

Owen Luder RIBA president (chair)

Sir Anthony Caro Sculptor

Hugh Pearman Architecture critic of *The Sunday Times*

Jane Priestman Chair of the RIBA Awards Group

.THE STIRLING PRIZE WINNER

.THE STIRLING PRIZE SHORTLIST

.THE STIRLING PRIZE 1996

THE CENTENARY BUILDING, UNIVERSITY OF SALFORD
.MANCHESTER
.HODDER ASSOCIATES
ALSO JOINT WINNER OF THE RIBA ARCHITECTURE IN EDUCATION AWARD

The Centenary Building is very much of its time, but it was also ahead of its time: it set trends and created a template for value-for-money academic buildings.

When setting the brief the client described the function of this building as a "fusion of design and technology" and asked that the building reflect this. The form is generated by the building's function but is also a response to its context, which is the threshold between the city and the academic campus. The result is a layered building in both plan and section, and it is this layering that gives it its special qualities.

The centre accommodates the departments of interior architecture, design studies, and graphic and industrial design, with a total of 400 students. Flexible studio and seminar space and three service towers are contained within a four-storey orthogonal 'bar' of accommodation defining the edge-of-the-city block. Prescribed tutorial accommodation and technology suites arranged in a free-form three-storey element face the newly defined courtyard.

The primary organizational device between the two types of accommodation is a linear atrium or 'street' within which all horizontal circulation via galleries is contained. In this way street life becomes a feature of the life of the building; common areas and adjoining offices and studios engage with the street, animating the building and imbuing it with a sense of purpose.

The first layer provides simple, flexible rectangular studios and seminar rooms. The second layer is a three-storey strip of cellular rooms for tutors. Behind these rooms is a third layer, the west-facing free-form structure that looks inwards towards the rest of the college, accommodating computer-aided design (CAD) suites, lecture theatres and studios.

Internally this building has a very special quality: the tall and narrow internal street is dynamic; top light washes down one side and is complemented by artificial light. Materials, detailing and colouring – grey, silver and white – are cool, and the asymmetry of its galleries and bridges creates patterns and

FIRST-FLOOR PLAN

CLIENT University of Salford STRUCTURAL ENGINEER Stephen Morley Partnership
CONTRACTOR AMEC Design and Management CONTRACT VALUE £3.6 million
PHOTOGRAPHER Dennis Gilbert – VIEW

a certain complexity. The result is light and lively. These qualities are reinforced by the architects' decision to deny some rooms windows, giving them instead fully glazed internal walls.

This is a building that responds in a symbolic and particular way to its brief and setting, but also one that succeeds in creating a whole that is both cool and crisp, dynamic and complex – a distinguished achievement.

Despite having been constructed quickly and cheaply (the team had to be on site just twelve weeks after appointment), the building is a modern and sophisticated exercise in steel, glass and concrete. The architects have bowed out the main façade to create a wide studio and lecture-theatre space with indirect daylighting, breaking the internal street with galleries and bridges, and exposing rooms to this central space to give an air of purpose and animation.

The chair of the Stirling jury, Owen Luder, commented: "The standard of entries this year demonstrates a high level of innovation and imagination across a range of building types, in particular in higher education. It is fascinating to see in the names of Morley, Hodder and Murphy the rise of a new and younger generation of architects. But Hodder's building is by far the most complex and ambitious and a worthy winner of the first Stirling Prize."

Hugh Pearman of *The Sunday Times* wrote: "One of the most successful Hodder projects of recent times, the multiple-award-winning Centenary Building at the University of Salford was designed and built with extreme rapidity by British standards. But it marked the most significant step forward yet for the practice, since the speed of its creation – combined with the clear need to create a new urban landmark to express the confidence of a new university – allowed Hodder a new freedom." Looking back ten years on, Stephen Hodder himself confessed: "Winning the Stirling Prize was amazing for the practice, but possibly it did come too early. Suddenly we were competing with the big boys like Hopkins at Nottingham University and MacCormac at Coventry. And we weren't really ready. In many ways it might have been better to win it later, when the prize itself had grown in status. Still, winning the first ever Stirling Prize was very special indeed for us."

PAGES 20–21 The Centenary Building does not look particularly radical today, but that is because of its success in setting a benchmark for all subsequent higher education buildings.

OPPOSITE The idea of the central street, a three-storey atrium with access to teaching rooms on the upper floors via walkways, is one successfully imported from commercial architecture.

RIGHT Stephen Hodder's building gives a sense of campus to what was previously a disparate collection of undistinguished teaching blocks.

D10 BUILDING, THE BOOTS COMPANY .NOTTINGHAM .AMEC DESIGN AND MANAGEMENT

WINNER OF THE RIBA DULUX HERITAGE COLOURS CONSERVATION AWARD

This innovative structure in reinforced concrete was designed in 1933 by Owen Williams, a master of glass and concrete, and is the largest Grade I-listed industrial building in the country. It was in a sorry state but has been painstakingly restored to as near as possible its original condition by its original client, while taking into account the company's changed operating requirements.

The project involved replacing all 3345 square metres of external glazing with new Crittall windows, replicating the old Crittall curtain walling; refurbishing five floors at the west end to provide laboratories on the ground floor, offices on three floors and a major plantroom in the basement, as well as the replacement and repair of the external building fabric and infrastructure. Design principles were established with English Heritage and two local planning authorities. These included that the mushroom-headed columns and original shuttering marks were to be left visible; the original functional appearance of the internal services was to remain; and the replacement windows not only had to reflect the character of the original ones, but also had to allow the internal columns to be clearly visible from the outside again, just as Williams had originally intended.

D10 was created to produce medicines, unlike D6 next door, which is a 'dry', churning out tablets. Dealing with a slice of history is never easy. D6, also built by Williams, is only slightly less important a building and is listed Grade II. It was mothballed twenty years ago because 'dry' production techniques could not match modern health standards. D10 faced the same fate. Demolition was out of the question, so the choice was either renovation or a £100 million bill for a new factory. However, preservation brought another headache. This is working history; any work would need to go on around a twenty-four-hour production process. The front of D10 was stripped and transformed to its original condition without production being halted in the rest of the building.

Initially, English Heritage wanted glazing reproduced exactly as built, but the steel frames are no longer made in the same way. So new frames were produced to modern standards by the original manufacturer, Crittall Windows, which managed to find a retired 1930s craftsman to offer advice. Tinted glass and internal blinds enabled the introduction of computer-based offices without problems of screen reflection. In the end English Heritage was happy to approve changes that matched the spirit of the building and kept it alive.

This is an impressive job, beautifully executed, relying on professional people who love their building. Even more impressively, it was procured under a design-and-management contract. It illustrates what can be done by a committed team.

ABOVE This is a fine example of conservation in action: the meticulous conservation of a Grade I-listed building without halting production on the rest of the site.

OPPOSITE It was not only the 3345 square metres of glass that needed to be replaced; Crittall, the original manufacturer, also had to make new frames to comply with modern standards.

CLIENT The Boots Company STRUCTURAL ENGINEER AMEC CONTRACTOR AMEC CONTRACT VALUE £20 million PHOTOGRAPHER Martine Hamilton Knight

MCC INDOOR CRICKET SCHOOL, LORD'S CRICKET GROUND .LONDON NW8 .DAVID MORLEY ARCHITECTS

WINNER OF THE RIBA ARCHITECTURE IN SPORT AND LEISURE AWARD

The conservative game of cricket and high-tech architecture may not at first seem natural bedfellows. There is precedent, however, not only here at Lord's in the shape of Michael Hopkins's Mound Stand – the scheme that brought Frei Otto-style tensile structures to the United Kingdom – but also in the clearly expressed structure of the majority of sports stands. Bringing together a surprisingly radical client and a moderately Modernist architect results in a crisp, elegant and practical solution.

The design of the indoor cricket school had to fit comfortably within the hierarchy of buildings on the site without competing visually with the main stands. The two principal ideas were the integration of all the cellular accommodation into a compact double-sided pavilion, and the containment of both the pavilion and the playing area within one envelope that lets in natural light in a controlled way. The school sits beside the nursery practice ground, across the south-east–north-west axis of the ground, so that it can operate without artificial light throughout daylight hours. The three-tube fluorescents, protected by cages and a retractable hanging net, are sufficiently powerful to allow

batsmen to see the fastest deliveries on to the bat during evening practice sessions. The lightness of the smooth aluminium roof obviates the need for up or down stands in the glazed or solid walls. The architects also specified powder-coated aluminium for the double-skin cladding instead of steel, because of its ability to resist without denting the impact of hard-driven cricket balls.

The building captures the spirit of its purpose. From the ingenuity of the plan to the well-considered sectional arrangement, colours and texture, it is legible and offers understanding about the way each component functions and relates both to other parts and to the whole. However, it is the roof that is the *tour de force*. An interpretation of the factory north-light roof, with the saw-tooth faces softened into curves to give better internal reflections, it takes the form of half-glazed barrel vaults. With fabric louvres underneath, these allow a wonderful quality of soft and even natural light to permeate the building. Full-height sliding doors roll back to allow practice to take place in a more natural cricketing environment.

ABOVE David Morley's work at Lord's, the shop as well as the cricket school, together with the work of Hopkins and Future Systems – with Grimshaw still to come – won the MCC the second RIBA Client of the Year Award in 1999.

OPPOSITE Morley's lightweight architecture is perfectly fit for the purpose of inserting new structures into the airy surroundings of a cricket ground.

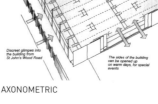

AXONOMETRIC

CLIENT Marylebone Cricket Club STRUCTURAL ENGINEER Price & Myers
CONTRACTOR Wates Construction (London) CONTRACT VALUE £2 million
PHOTOGRAPHER Dennis Gilbert – VIEW

PROCTER & GAMBLE HEADQUARTERS
.WEYBRIDGE, SURREY .AUKETT ASSOCIATES
WINNER OF THE RIBA COMMERCIAL ARCHITECTURE AWARD

This is an imposing new headquarters building on the site of the old Brooklands racing track. The project provides a three-phase total of 23,225 square metres of office accommodation including conference and restaurant facilities. The client's brief asked that the building should encourage good communication and teamwork and be open, welcoming, light and constructed with good-quality materials. The first phase, which accommodates 530 staff, is arranged as two three-storey wings on either side of a central glazed atrium. At the upper levels the offices are open to the atrium, creating the sense of the building being one space and encouraging a feeling of corporate belonging. The atrium, engineered by Tony Hunt, houses the reception area, staff shop, coffee bar and central landscaped arena for informal meetings and break-time conversation space, as well as the lifts and internal staircases, making for a single-space headquarters in both physical and corporate terms.

The building is clad in powder-coated aluminium-framed curtain walling; it incorporates sunshade louvres, limestone spandrels and vertical stone panels. The use of clear glass with passive solar control underlines the general design philosophy of a translucent, light building that maximizes inside/outside awareness. The double-glazed atrium roof, measuring 41 metres by 22 metres, is supported on laminated-glass fin purlins that are in turn supported by curved steel trusses. The dramatic three-storey glazed end walls are held in place by bowstring trusses. The use of lightweight tubular steel contributes to transparency, increases light levels and determines the aesthetic of the building.

Two steel bridges, each 18 metres long, support the impressive three-storey helical staircase. The bridges consist of steel-plate decks supported on tubular lattice trusses, with additional support provided by suspension rods secured from roof level. Floors within the bridges are screed-filled and carpeted.

This is a light, crisply detailed modern building in a well-landscaped setting. Light, modern materials have been used throughout, with a predominance of glass, which has been well detailed. It sets new standards of design for corporate headquarters buildings.

ABOVE This *urbs in rures* project set new design standards for corporate headquarters, and its shortlisting encouraged other commercial clients to be more adventurous in their commissioning.

OPPOSITE The architects have addressed the problems of solar gain, which are always associated with largely glazed buildings, with a passive solar-control system, supplemented by brises-soleil and blinds.

CLIENT Procter & Gamble – Health and Beautycare **STRUCTURAL ENGINEERS** Aukett Associates/Anthony Hunt Associates **CONTRACTOR** Costain Construction **CONTRACT VALUE** £20 million **PHOTOGRAPHERS** Peter Cook – VIEW (opposite)/ Timothy Soar (above)

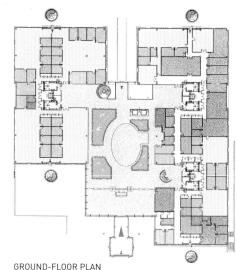

GROUND-FLOOR PLAN

THE QUEEN'S BUILDING, EMMANUEL COLLEGE .CAMBRIDGE .MICHAEL HOPKINS AND PARTNERS

JOINT WINNER OF THE RIBA ARCHITECTURE IN EDUCATION AWARD

Michael Hopkins and Partners' contribution to both gown and town in Cambridge (it addresses the street far more than it does the college buildings) is understated, almost self-effacing. It also looks far more traditional in its construction than it really is.

The building provides a new lecture and performance space for the college, seating 150 people, with a raked auditorium and a surrounding gallery. The acoustic, primarily designed for chamber music and small orchestral groups, is adjustable for lectures and for cinema and theatre performances. At the upper levels, other accommodation includes a reception room for use with the auditorium and a new Middle Common Room. A quiet reading room and a number of small seminar and music-practice rooms are entered from an open colonnade that rings the building at ground level.

A striking aspect of this building is the sense it has of the ancient in the modern. This derives not merely from its use of Ketton limestone (the same material Wren used for the college's chapel) for the primary structure; it resides also in the elemental quality that has been distilled out of what is a complex modern fabric. Both the very high budget and the architects' and engineers' skill have clearly been essential to making the complex appear simple. As a material, stone is weak in tension and needs to be reinforced in some way. The obvious way would have been to use buttresses; instead, each of the building's twenty-eight stone columns contains a stainless steel rod, accessed through stainless steel roundels, giving a high-tech touch to a low-tech building. Movement is accommodated by using lime mortar instead of cement. Windows are flush at first- and second-floor levels; only on the ground floor are they recessed to give that shady colonnade.

Although the curved concrete staircase, detailed with American white oak, has a cool beauty to it, the auditorium is the most important internal space and is brilliantly successful both spatially and in use. Stainless steel and hardwood dominate. Together with the jewellery-like fineness of detailing, they create a sense that one is inside a musical instrument. Acoustics are enhanced not only by the heavy masonry structure but also by the lead-lined roof, a device previously used by the practice in the Glyndebourne Opera House. This building also shares with Glyndebourne an unfussy design throughout the auditorium.

This is a fine building, in the understated Oxbridge collegiate tradition of MacCormac and Cullinan.

ABOVE, BELOW AND OPPOSITE BOTTOM This is a high-tech building in low-tech clothes; the heavy masonry hides a number of clever structural devices.

OPPOSITE TOP Internally, the architects and engineers have combined to produce one of the finest acoustics in the country, refining their earlier work together at Glyndebourne.

CLIENT Emmanuel College, University of Cambridge STRUCTURAL ENGINEER Buro Happold CONTRACTOR Sir Robert McAlpine CONTRACT VALUE £4.3 million PHOTOGRAPHER Dennis Gilbert – VIEW

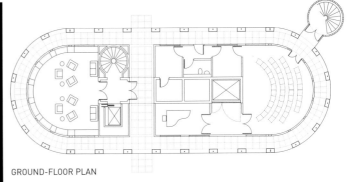

GROUND-FLOOR PLAN

17 ROYAL TERRACE MEWS
.EDINBURGH .RICHARD MURPHY ARCHITECTS
WINNER OF THE RIBA IBSTOCK AWARD FOR HOUSES AND HOUSING

Unlike many Edinburgh mews properties, this former stable and hayloft dating from the 1820s had not been converted to residential use when the client commissioned Richard Murphy to make it into a one-bedroom flat for rent. The conversion is intended to express the idea of a new house found within the repaired shell of the existing stable so that the history of the building is conveyed, particularly on the front façade. In effect, the architects have accepted the structure for what it is, and made a building within a building.

To obtain planning permission, a garage was required, so the internal floor level has been changed to create the main living space upstairs. The lowered first floor is expressed on the front elevation in a steel channel that also forms the runner for the garage door. The asymmetric planar language of the new architecture finds expression in panels of glass block and lead on this façade, the latter appearing to form an inner skin behind the stone, although in reality they are dressed either into shadow gaps or mirrors. Internally the lead masks two internal panels that close down the whole front façade at night.

By day the dramatic glass-ridge roof light lets in all the light that is needed. This is achieved by arranging the spaces in a sequence to follow the path of the sun around the flat: in the morning the sun strikes the bed; during the course of the day it reflects down the north wall into the kitchen; and in the evening it casts a beam across the living-room wall. Internally, mirrors are placed under the ridge to extend the space laterally and to throw light around the room. This single act brings all the necessary extra light into the property while maintaining the integrity of the uninterrupted slate roofs.

Within the space there are moving doors that can close or half-close some areas. Much of the furniture, including wardrobes, desk and even the bed, was designed as part of the commission.

Hugh Pearman has described Richard Murphy's work as maximalist; certainly there is a richness about it, in terms of both materials and invention. This is a remarkable piece of pocket-sized architecture – a delightful little building, full of imaginative touches and clever detailing that confirm the skill and inventiveness of the architects.

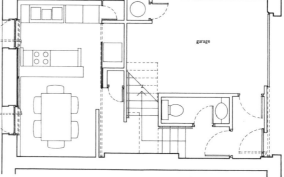

GROUND-FLOOR PLAN

CLIENT Carol Høgel STRUCTURAL ENGINEER David Narro Associates
CONTRACTOR Inscape Joinery CONTRACT VALUE £190,000 PHOTOGRAPHERS Alan Forbes (opposite)/Gavin Fraser (above)

ABOVE Richard Murphy was so pleased with this box of tricks that he rented it himself when his client put it on the rental market a few years after the award was made.

OPPOSITE This is very much a new build within an old building. Only the glass blocks on the stable's façade hint at the sophisticated interior.

THE STIRLING PRIZE 1996
.HUGH PEARMAN
ARCHITECTURE CRITIC OF *THE SUNDAY TIMES*

We chose a bummer of a year in which to launch a prize for architecture that was meant to rival the Turner Prize for contemporary art. The year was a very lean one for good new buildings in the United Kingdom. Architecture was only just starting to climb out of a long, deep economic recession. We were too late to catch the crop of big projects begun in the 1980s and finished during the downturn: Nicholas Grimshaw's Eurostar terminal at Waterloo, Michael Hopkins's Glyndebourne Opera House, Richard Rogers's Channel 4 headquarters, say. And for this shoestring first outing we confined ourselves to the United Kingdom, so we couldn't fall back on the work of British architects elsewhere in Europe.

Meanwhile, the Lottery-fuelled riches of the Millennium, although starting to emerge on paper, were years from completion. Because of the expectations heaped on the new prize, not to mention the blithe assurances I had given my editor when persuading him to part with £20,000 in sponsorship money, I remember starting to feel slightly desperate. Still, nothing ventured ...

At least the field was wide open. Some promising new talents were starting to emerge. When I discussed the prize with Mary Stirling, she had been keen on the idea of younger architects getting a boost from the award: something that would have been hugely helpful to Jim Stirling when he was starting up in the 1950s. So we had the interesting prospect of the first Stirling Prize going to a non-Establishment name, and that was good.

Apart from the up-and-comers, there was another aspect to the goods on offer in 1996. Compared to the 1970s and 1980s, the chasm between the signature practices and the mainstream was narrowing. The base standard was starting to rise. This too was potentially good. But we couldn't give the first Stirling Prize to a merely OK building. It had to be excellent.

Our raw material was the longlist provided by the regional winners of the RIBA Awards. This was whittled down to an official shortlist of what were called 'category winners', an unwieldy typological concept that was later dropped. When drawing up this shortlist, we had the power to call in buildings if we thought they had been overlooked or under-rated in the regional heats. This was a lifeline, not only in the first year, but also later. There was a lot of riffling through the rejects heap. Were we overlooking some hidden gem somewhere? After the usual horse-trading, the contenders were finalized.

So off we judges set: Sir Anthony Caro, sculptor; Owen Luder, RIBA president; and me. We were organized by Chris Palmer, the RIBA's shrewd and unfailingly cheerful director of communications. In fact, Jane Priestman, a great patron of architecture and chair of the Awards Group, deputized for Owen, who was off sick for much of the process. This meant that the first Stirling Prize was essentially decided by non-architects. Amazingly, nobody made a fuss about this. Not in public, anyway.

We had a shortlist of six, refined from an original entry of 381 to the RIBA Awards. And looking back on them now, they were not only a bit of a rum bunch; they would have been hard-pressed to get on to the Stirling shortlist in later years. They were the product of a period of lower ambition than we have now become used to. But wasn't that the point of the prize – to raise everyone's sights?

The six were:

- the glassy high tech of the Procter & Gamble HQ in Weybridge by Aukett Associates;
- the sculpturally assured Centenary Building at the University of Salford by Hodder Associates, housing a design faculty;
- the Queen's Building at Emmanuel College, University of Cambridge, by Michael Hopkins and Partners, an oval stone building containing a small theatre and common room;
- the immaculate whites of the MCC Indoor Cricket School at Lord's by David Morley Architects, which happened to have been the building where we launched the prize;
- a small, highly crafted mews house conversion by Richard Murphy in Edinburgh;
- the restoration of Owen Williams's Grade I-listed 1933 Boots factory in Nottingham by Jan Sosna and others of AMEC Design and Management.

So we had three rising younger names (Hodder, Morley and Murphy), one big-hitting signature architect (Hopkins) and two commercial outfits (Aukett and AMEC).

The Hopkins was an odd and somehow unnecessary little bull-nosed structure from his heavyweight period. Procter & Gamble was a good stab at the high-tech aesthetic, but did not innovate. The refit of the Boots building was a bit naff. So it was always going to come down to one of the three from the new generation.

A small house conversion – although intelligent and imaginative as always from Murphy – was not Stirling material. That left Hodder and Morley, and this was close. Morley's cricket school was basically an elegant big barrel-vaulted shed with rooms and a bar attached. All nicely carried through, although it turned its back rather pointedly on a key London urban corner. Another Lord's building, by Future Systems, was to strike gold three years later.

That left Hodder's Centenary Building at Salford. Hodder had been working for years on his student housing for St Catherine's College, Oxford, while this job was, in contrast, super-fast and done with a lighter touch. It expressed the ambitions of what was a new combined university in the middle of a deprived area. Its proportions, muscular tectonics and use of an almost industrial aesthetic in the full-height internal street showed remarkable confidence.

Politically, the Centenary Building had a lot going for it: a promising young northern architect and a low-cost building that was a fine piece of architecture and something of a catalyst for regeneration, well away from the southern bastions of privilege. Oh, and its glimmering curving silver flanks photographed very well. We had our winner. Would it even make it on to today's Stirling shortlist? Probably not. Today, post-Millennium, the bar is much higher and the net is much wider. But in 1996 it gave out a message of hope. As the famous pop anthem had it during the general election of the following year, things could only get better.

.JUDGES

David Rock RIBA president (chair)
Marco Goldschmied Director of Richard Rogers Partnership
and chair of the RIBA Awards Group
Stephen Hodder Architect and Stirling Prize winner in 1996
Hugh Pearman Architecture critic of *The Sunday Times*
Charles Saumarez Smith Director of the National Portrait Gallery

.THE STIRLING PRIZE WINNER

.THE STIRLING PRIZE SHORTLIST

.THE STIRLING PRIZE 1997

THE MUSIC SCHOOL .STUTTGART, GERMANY .MICHAEL WILFORD AND PARTNERS

ALSO JOINT WINNER OF THE RIBA ARCHITECTURE IN EDUCATION AWARD

This was the last building Sir James Stirling worked on before his death in 1992. The designs were completed by his partner, Michael Wilford, and other members of the partnership. The Music School and the History Museum (then under construction) complete the sequence of public buildings in the urban masterplan conceived for Stuttgart's 'Cultural Mile' flanking Konrad-Adenauer-Strasse, and continue the series of external semi-enclosed spaces opening towards the city initiated by the adjacent Staatsgalerie. A new raised plaza, framed by the Music School, History Museum and existing Landtag building, is the focus of the composition.

The Music School has nine floors with accommodation for students and public. The chamber music/lecture hall and the 450-seat concert hall and library are located in a tower on the plaza, marking the presence of the Music School on the city's skyline. Entrance is via a four-storey foyer that provides multiple connections as well as acting as the main public vestibule. There is also accommodation for departments of music theory, composition and pitch, practice and teaching rooms, and a senate room with its own roof-top terrace for receptions or small concerts.

The Music School may not make the most striking photographs, but to see it is to realize what a magnificent building it is. It is a powerful piece of architecture by architects working at the height of their powers. Its general form was first published many years earlier, and, for a design that has been around for a long time, the realization is no disappointment: there is still an impression of astonishing originality, and the details remain fresh and free from cliché.

The building is a Classically inspired work of great power and subtlety that can be directly compared to the work of the interwar Scandinavian master Gunnar Asplund. The battered and perforated cylinder of the tower is ranged against, and cut into, the rectilinear block of the main building, setting up a tension that is resolved with exceptional clarity within, right down to the arrangement of the pipes in the great organ in the flamboyantly colourful concert hall, above which is the library with its double-height perimeter and giant-scale bookshelves. It is a building that both surprises and inspires.

The Music School is unusual in being a late example of the neglected British monumental tradition. This architectural strand runs in the twentieth century from Lutyens, through Spence to Lasdun and Stirling, and from Stirling to his long-term professional partner, Wilford. Massive, beautifully made and ingeniously sited, the Music School is of a quality that is rare anywhere in the United Kingdom.

PAGE 38 The tapered drum houses the principal functions of the Music School – concert hall and library – and culminates in a spectacular roof-top terrace.

PAGE 39 The concert hall presented Michael Wilford with a canvas on which to demonstrate his flamboyant use of colour.

ABOVE With the Music School, James Stirling's original masterplan was two-thirds complete; only the History Museum (RIBA Award winner in 2003) remained to be built.

OPPOSITE The servicing ducts in the concert hall are every bit as sculptural as the organ pipes that they flank.

CLIENT Land Baden-Württemberg STRUCTURAL ENGINEERS Ove Arup & Partners/ Boll und Partner CONTRACTOR Wolff & Müller CONTRACT VALUE DM90 million PHOTOGRAPHER Richard Bryant – Arcaid

Kenneth Powell wrote in 1993: "James Stirling was, at the time of his death in 1992, perhaps the most famous and most revered architect in the world – he was also one of the most widely misunderstood and misrepresented, even by many of his admirers. He attracted admiration in plenty but created no school of design. His practice, in the safe hands of Michael Wilford, will go on to enrich the world of the future. The atelier in Fitzroy Square, where the memories are strong, the music always plays and the tea never ceases to flow, will be a powerhouse of the architecture of the spirit and the heart for a long time to come." This award shows how accurate that prediction was. Accepting the award in November 1997, Wilford brandished the trophy and declared, "This is for Jim."

LE GRAND BLEU (REGIONAL GOVERNMENT HEADQUARTERS)
.MARSEILLES, FRANCE .ALSOP & STÖRMER
WINNER OF THE RIBA CIVIC AND COMMUNITY ARCHITECTURE AWARD

The Hôtel du Département in Marseilles, known locally as
Le Grand Bleu, was completed in 1994. This headquarters for
the Département des Bouches-du-Rhône was deliberately
sited on the edge of a poor quarter of the city, although it is
only four stations from the centre on the Métro that stops
outside the door. Its regenerative impact is seen in an old
petrol station that has been converted into a smart restaurant
nearby. It has been described by *The Guardian*'s architecture
correspondent, Jonathan Glancey, as "a huge, dramatic, wave-
like, Yves Klein-blue sofa of regional government. Charismatic
and eventful, it attracts a million visitors a year, who gawp
at it in much the same way as tourists gawp at Frank Gehry's
Bilbao Guggenheim."

The heart of the building is a void, an immense atrium that
makes the building transparent and, by implication, accessible.
The offices, housing 7000 staff in 100,000 square metres, are in
two long rectangular blocks of seven and nine storeys on either
side of this atrium. A free-standing elliptical tube (more than a
little reminiscent of the practice's Cardiff Bay Visitor Centre)
provides public exhibition space. With their moveable walls, the
offices are designed to be flexible. The three lower floors are
double- and triple-height spaces, defined by X-shaped columns,
and accommodate a mediathèque, library and cafeteria. Of the
two externally visible ovoid forms, the one on top of the taller
block (the Aerofoil) accommodates the offices of directors
and councillors, while the other (the Délibératif) houses two
debating chambers.

The client, director of architecture Pierre Garnier, insisted
on an international competition in a city where most of the public-
sector work went to two politically well-connected practices:
"We didn't want a little provincial building; we wanted to show the
technology and architecture of the twenty-first century." It took
three rounds to separate Will Alsop from Norman Foster (after
the other 154 proposals had been eliminated), but two factors
were crucial so far as the council president was concerned:
Alsop shared both his love of fly-fishing and his jovial manner.

With its vivid blue glass skin, Le Grand Bleu makes a
majestic landmark in this poor area, looming above the soft-
red pantiles like an alien spacecraft, the occupants of which
have decided that life on the Mediterranean coast beats that on
their own planet. In transition from competition to execution,
the programme in some ways got the better of the formal intent.
But the powerful forms and dramatic spaces of Le Grand Bleu
are genuinely moving: they affirm the power of architecture and
express the confidence and optimism of Département 13 and the
cosmopolitanism and vigour of Marseilles.

BELOW There is a generosity of scale to the interiors that would be unthinkable
in a public building in the United Kingdom.

OPPOSITE The blue glass structure pre-dated Peter Cook's Graz Kunsthaus
by almost a decade but attracted similar comparisons to alien spacecraft.

CLIENT Conseil Général des Bouches-du-Rhône STRUCTURAL ENGINEER Ove Arup
& Partners CONTRACT VALUE FF883.5 million PHOTOGRAPHER Roderick Coyne

LONDON UNDERGROUND STRATFORD MARKET DEPOT .LONDON E15 .CHRIS WILKINSON ARCHITECTS

WINNER OF THE RIBA COMMERCIAL ARCHITECTURE AWARD

Chris Wilkinson specializes in structural-engineering solutions to architectural problems, and here, at the back-end of Stratford, the problems were legion. The depot, on an 11-hectare site previously used by British Rail as sidings, is intended to provide maintenance for all fifty-nine trains on the extended Jubilee line. The precise location of the maintenance shed was determined by the discovery of the remains of a medieval abbey at the east of the site, pushing the shed to the other end. But here the need to straighten up the curved tracks before they enter the shed meant that the front elevation had to be sliced through 30 degrees. So the distinctive rhomboid shape, far from being a design whim, is a practical response to a tricky problem. The parallelogram shape also determined a non-orthogonal grid for the space-frame roof structure.

The functions of the shed fall into three distinct zones that are reflected by having just two rows of columns on a grid measuring 18 metres by 42 metres. These concrete-filled steel columns act as vertical cantilever trees that connect at three points to the space grid. An abundance of natural light is provided to the shed via a fully glazed end wall and translucent panels to the rear elevation. Further roof slots make the building an important marker for aircraft stacking in their approach to Heathrow Airport. Down on the ground, the calm ambience is enhanced by the pale green steelwork.

Elsewhere on the site, the brief called for outdoor stabling for thirty-three trains. The trains' movements are monitored from a circular control tower with views over the shed and workshops. In a bleak industrial landscape this building stands out as a landmark. The trains inside are the subject of a form of maintenance contract with the train manufacturer that requires higher performance levels than those previously achieved within London Underground. None of this would have been possible without this exemplary building. It has made a fitting contribution to standards of efficiency. Moreover, in its external appearance and quality of working environment, it is an enjoyable place to work.

In choice of materials and minute attention to detail the Stratford depot sets new standards for this building type; yet in its back-street, all but railway-locked, location it is seen by virtually no one. However, in Roland Paoletti, London Underground's architect/client, it had a champion who was both demanding and inspiring, and, as Chris Wilkinson says, "This was the first Jubilee line project to be finished, so it established the status and importance of the whole project."

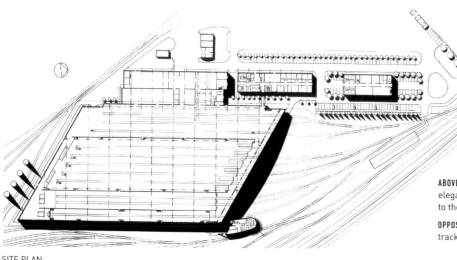

SITE PLAN

ABOVE After the whimsy of Wilford and Alsop, the judges appreciated the simple elegance of this working building. Even the parallelogram shape is a response to the constraints of the site.

OPPOSITE The 30-degree angle of the entrance façade allows the curve of the tracks to be straightened for ease of train maintenance.

CLIENT LUL Jubilee Line Extension Project Team **STRUCTURAL ENGINEER** Hyder Consulting **MAIN CONTRACTOR** John Laing Construction **CONTRACT VALUE** £18 million **PHOTOGRAPHER** Dennis Gilbert – VIEW

MAGGIE KESWICK JENCKS CANCER CARING CENTRE
.EDINBURGH .RICHARD MURPHY ARCHITECTS
WINNER OF THE RIBA ARCHITECTURE IN HEALTHCARE AWARD

The Cancer Caring Centre at Edinburgh's Western General Hospital was inspired by the late Maggie Jencks, wife of Charles, who died of cancer in 1995. Her vision, which she encapsulated in a detailed brief and constitution, was for a place where those diagnosed with cancer could get help and information and have access to massage, yoga, individual counselling and group sessions on such issues as nutrition and healthcare. On Maggie's death, her former nurse, Laura Lee, took on the role of championing the project.

At the suggestion of film-maker Murray Grigor, Charles Jencks looked at Richard Murphy's work when setting out to find his architect. He was impressed by the way Murphy cared about the smallest detail and was able to mix old and new codes of architecture, bringing out the subtleties of each. Jencks has described Murphy as "a jeweller of the small, in the manner of his hero Carlo Scarpa, creative in his use of small space and indirect light".

Since the aim from the outset was to create an air of therapeutic domesticity, in contrast to the inevitably institutional nature of the accommodation for surgical and medical treatment, the building donated by the hospital was perfect. The former stable block, then being used as a garden store, incorporated two large stable doors and a hayloft; these have been retained and a

flexible building constructed inside. The double-height entrance is full of light from a ridge roof light. Two staircases lead to the upper counselling and therapy rooms. People using the centre (the families of sufferers as much as the patients themselves) can sit on the stairs or on cushions as they consult the reference books from the shelves on the staircases. The four individual rooms are capable of being combined by means of sliding and folding doors, producing a large hall for presentations, meetings or even dinners.

The exterior has a robust austerity; the inside is full of surprise and delight, a remarkably expansive, even luminous space. Philosophically, the centre is all about patient empowerment through information, and the architect has responded by placing this element physically as well as symbolically at the heart of the building. By contrast to the somewhat grand hall, the more domestic parts are appropriately quiet in character: white walls and timber finishes produce an atmosphere of calm in the living-room, dining-room and kitchen.

The idea for the centre comes from California, yet it seems entirely at home in the grounds of a Scottish NHS hospital. The building has subsequently been doubled in size by the same architect and has been a model for other similar centres in the United Kingdom.

RIGHT Richard Murphy's detailing, far from being overwhelming, has a calming, even therapeutic effect.

OPPOSITE As with his previously shortlisted mews house, Murphy has taken a stable block and, working in an identical language, produced an inspiring building, entirely fit for purpose.

CLIENT Maggie's Centre Trust STRUCTURAL ENGINEER David Narro Associates
MAIN CONTRACTOR Peter Moran CONTRACT VALUE £127,900 PHOTOGRAPHER Alan Forbes

PAUL HAMLYN LEARNING RESOURCE CENTRE, THAMES VALLEY UNIVERSITY .SLOUGH, BERKSHIRE .RICHARD ROGERS PARTNERSHIP

JOINT WINNER OF THE RIBA ARCHITECTURE IN EDUCATION AWARD

The architects were asked to masterplan a new learning centre, including a landscape strategy and plans for future expansion. The site was previously occupied by an engineering workshop dating from the 1950s. The brief called for two spaces over a total area of 3500 square metres: one an open working environment that encouraged interaction on the ground and mezzanine levels, the other an information warehouse or bookstack on three storeys. Both were to be united under a lightweight, curved roof. The roof projects at the southern end to form the entrance. A third element is the surrounding landscape. Vice-chancellor Mike Fitzgerald's brief also called for "a new model in higher education, putting students at the fore and freeing them from an education where time and space are constraints. The building and facilities within [should] encourage students to study at their own pace, in their own time, using a variety of learning styles."

The rectilinear three-storey bookstack has an *in situ* fair-faced concrete frame and uses its thermal mass, as well as opening windows, to reduce the need for mechanical ventilation. However, natural ventilation is impossible in the internal seminar rooms and in the main hall, where more than a hundred computer terminals make air conditioning a necessity.

The Learning Resource Centre featured in a 1996 BBC series looking at the commissioning and construction process. The series showed the young project architects getting a hard time from a wily client but demonstrated in the end that the practice's approach to design can still deal with small buildings on reasonable budgets and that good design does not need to cost the earth.

The judges found a refreshing simplicity in the form and structure of this building. The main study space has a generosity that is both uplifting and warm. The use of colour is fun without being garish, and the quality of light and the shadows it casts create endless surprises. This is a low-cost building where money has been spent sparingly and only where it will have most benefit, as in the main glass stair. The choice of simple, robust and naturally finished materials is highly successful and adds to the clarity and sense of purpose of the building. The LRC has become, in the client's words, "the electronic hub of the university and surrounding communities, linking TVU to the wider global community and facilitating the very best practices in both education and business". Not bad for a building with such a modest budget and on such a tight site.

ABOVE This shed for learning is low cost (£3.6 million), with the money being spent only where it has the most impact.

RIGHT The university is proud of its Rogers building, which stood as a beacon for an expanding higher education sector.

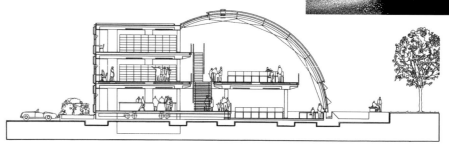

CLIENT Thames Valley University **STRUCTURAL ENGINEER** Buro Happold
MAIN CONTRACTOR John Laing Construction **CONTRACT VALUE** £3.6 million
PHOTOGRAPHER Katsuhisa Kida

SECTION

ROOF-TOP APARTMENT
.PARIS, FRANCE .MARK GUARD ARCHITECTS
WINNER OF THE RIBA HOUSES AND HOUSING AWARD

The client purchased a small single-storey building that sat on top of a large expanse of flat roof above an eight-storey 1930s apartment building in Paris's fifth arrondissement. The flat is reached via an old-fashioned cage lift and an obstacle course of a roof.

Measuring just 8 metres by 4 metres, this is a real Tardis of a structure. Despite the challenging dimensions, the brief called for a separate bedroom, so architect Mark Guard looked at planning arrangements that could maintain the full visual dimensions of the envelope. The brief was further complicated by the likelihood that friends and relatives would want to stay. Guard has used three free-standing boxes, a pivoting door and a number of sliding doors to produce a transformable space. The bedroom can be open-plan or separated if there are guests. A sofa bed in the living space provides accommodation for the occasional guest. The bathroom can be *en suite* to the bedroom or accessed from the living space. The free-standing boxes contain wardrobes, a television, washing machine, fridge and towel hanger, with the towels being exposed when the bathroom door is shut. A storage wall surrounds the stainless steel kitchen, the worktop projecting into the bathroom separated by 'Priva-lite'

glass. Closing the bathroom door activates the glass, turning it from clear to opaque.

The west wall of the building has been replaced by a folding glass wall and glass canopy. The canopy allows the doors to remain open in the summer rain. A French limestone floor is laid throughout the apartment and taken out on to the terrace, where there are spectacular views of the historic core of Paris.

Modern technology allows the client, whose main residence is in London, to activate the underfloor heating and the water heaters by telephone before he arrives in Paris. Electronically controlled metal shutters secure the building when he is away.

This very small apartment is a complete delight. It is as thoroughly well thought through and as well built as a boat cabin. The attention to detail is impressive, the spaces within the tiny volume capable of being arranged with ease in a number of configurations, even to the extent of putting up guests with a surprising degree of privacy. Many elements have more than one function, yet the apartment is mostly self-explanatory in use. This is a very unusual and highly successful urban eyrie.

RIBA Journal editor John Welsh commented: "[Guard] turns the typical dumb, minimalist space into something sculptural."

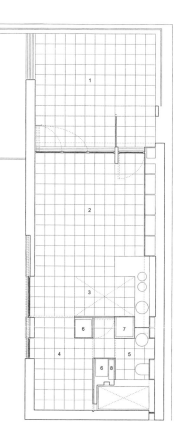

ABOVE Mark Guard's tiny apartment sails above the roofscapes of Paris.

OPPOSITE The flat is as packed with clever details as a narrowboat; sliding doors save space and ensure maximum flexibility.

PLAN

CLIENT Private STRUCTURAL ENGINEER Michael Baigent Orla Kelly MAIN CONTRACTOR Metrotech & Co. CONTRACT VALUE £118,440 PHOTOGRAPHER Jacques Crenn

THE STIRLING PRIZE 1997
.MARCUS BINNEY
ARCHITECTURE CORRESPONDENT OF *THE TIMES*

The perennial question with the Stirling Prize is whether the judges were right. Did the pressures of the moment prompt the wrong choice? In 1997 they started with an exceptional shortlist of exciting projects by good architects and the balance of large and small projects that gives younger architects a chance to share the stage.

I went to the opening of the Richard Rogers Partnership's Paul Hamlyn Centre in Slough. Tony Blair, newly elected, glided round, winning even more rapt attention than the building. The building is classic Rogers, a glorious space, lofty, open and filled with light, glowing with colour, and with the engineering boldly on display. It was the perfect metaphor for the new government's ambitions, a positive inspiration for Cool Britannia and far better than some of what followed.

I found Will Alsop's Grand Bleu mesmerizing. Although I never got the lunch I'd been promised by Alsop, the building was more than worth the journey and the hell-raising taxi ride. Both form and colour are overwhelmingly intense in the strong midday sun. Given the way the building evolved from Alsop's decidedly homespun models, with the debating chamber looking like a soggy cigar, the crispness of line and form was thrilling. So were the public spaces both inside and out. For me it remains his very best building.

Chris Wilkinson's Stratford Market depot confirmed the practice's place among the fastest-rising stars in British architecture. It shows the practice's phenomenal capacity to bring fresh thinking and elegant line and form to everything it does. At a time when every town in England was being surrounded by crass boxes containing discount stores and warehousing, Wilkinson invented the supershed. Here was a vast covered space that looked sleek, lean and low, with much of its beauty deriving from its mastery of the gently unravelling eyelid curve. This is surely the longest and lowest Wilkinson has produced, the opposite of the steeply rising arch of the moving-eye bridge over the Tyne.

In Stuttgart, Michael Wilford had the task of adding to Stirling's art gallery, at that time as revered an icon as Gehry's Guggenheim. Stirling's late work made astonishing play with monumental geometric forms. On occasion this became obsessive, as at Glyndebourne, which he lost to Michael Hopkins, partly because the purity of geometry took precedence over responding to the client's brief, effectively putting him out of the running. At Stuttgart the geometry succeeds on a grand scale. Stirling used to say the Music School tower was the positive of the negative represented by the art gallery courtyard. "The cork has jumped out of the bottle", he joked.

Wilford was developing a concept begun by Stirling, but the completed building has all the hallmarks of practicality and engaging friendliness that infuse Wilford's work. He cleverly adapted the monumental geometry to a much more complicated building with 120 rehearsal rooms for individuals and groups. By giving the rooms a tapering form he avoided the parallax that can be a problem while rehearsing. Musicians, he says with some justice, often have opposing views on acoustics. Here there is an adjustable acoustic panel on one wall of each room. Ceilings are also treated to avoid reflections.

Wilford, like Alsop, makes virtuoso use of colour. Within, the concert hall glows with red and golden yellow, contrasting with the regal purple immediately outside. At a time when all-glass walls were favoured even for buildings to which they were quite unsuited, Wilford here proclaims the traditional virtues of solid mass interspersed with windows, although these are given a distinctive look by the bold glazing pattern.

Mark Guard was making his name with ingenious minimalist conversions and extensions to standard terrace houses. His roof-top apartment in the rue Tournefort on top of a 1930s apartment block in the fifth arrondissement was as neatly planned and detailed as a yacht cabin. With a build cost of £118,440, it could never compare with Wilford's DM90 million Music School or Alsop's FF883.5 million, but shortlisting gave deserved recognition to a young architect who devotes intense skill and ingenuity to even the most modest projects.

Richard Murphy designed the first of the now-renowned Maggie's Centres (contract value £127,900). Sitting in the grounds of Edinburgh's Western General Hospital, the centre has been installed in the former stable block and retains the large stable doors and hayloft. Murphy was the first to realize Maggie Jencks's vision for places of solace where cancer patients could both come to terms with illness and gather the strength to fight it.

I would have awarded the Stirling Prize to Alsop. His is a masterpiece, bold, original, a major landmark, with new works by artists woven into it to create the proverbial total work of art out of a very functional and public civic building. One reason given to Alsop (unofficially) for his rejection was that part of the interior was not his: the Salon d'honneur in the Délibératif had been handed to an interior decorator. But then quite a proportion of the office floors at 30 St Mary Axe were given to other designers whose work (in my view) detracts from Foster's superb internal volumes.

Yet the wheel comes round. Alsop was on the shortlist again in 1999 with his aqueous blue Underground station at North Greenwich and won with his Peckham Library in 2000. He also pipped Wilford in the competition for the West Bromwich Arts Centre.

By contrast, Wilford and his German partner, Manuel Schupp, have the best form of satisfaction. Their building continues to impress its users. The most handsome recent tribute was paid by the composer Yueyang Wang, born and trained in Beijing but now living and working in Germany. When asked to name her favourite performing spaces, she replied: "My work is performed in galleries, on the street, in churches, parks, grand stair halls and classic concert halls. For its good acoustic I would choose the Stuttgart Music School."

1 9 6 8

.JUDGES

David Rock RIBA president (chair)

James Dyson Designer and industrialist

Marco Goldschmied Chair of the RIBA Awards Group

Hugh Pearman Architecture critic of *The Sunday Times*

Michael Wilford Stirling Prize winner in 1997

.THE STIRLING PRIZE WINNER

.THE STIRLING PRIZE SHORTLIST

.THE STIRLING PRIZE 1998

AMERICAN AIR MUSEUM IN BRITAIN, IMPERIAL WAR MUSEUM .DUXFORD, CAMBRIDGE .FOSTER AND PARTNERS
ALSO JOINT WINNER OF THE RIBA SPORT AND LEISURE AWARD

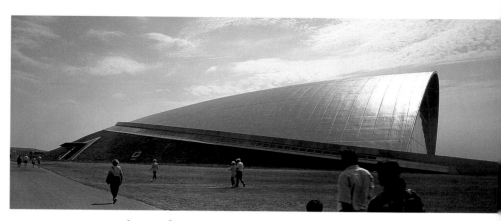

In 1986 Foster and Partners was asked by the Imperial War Museum to design a museum to house its collection of American World War II aircraft that had flown from East Anglian bases, including Duxford. Visitors approach through a tunnel-like entrance and find themselves facing the nose of a B-52 Stratofortress so large that its shape determined the form of the building. The dramatically curved roof is partially dug into the landscape, and the abrupt slice of the building's façade, measuring 90 metres by 18.5 metres, gives sweeping views on to the runway. This glass wall is fully demountable, allowing aircraft to be rolled in and out of the museum. The roof soars to accommodate the B-52's 16-metre tail fin, and its 61-metre wingspan means the wings all but tip the sides of the building. Other aircraft stand around it or are hung from suspension points in the ceiling. Even though they weigh up to 10 tonnes each, they look like toys against the mass of the B-52, that chilling symbol of the Cold War.

Crucial to the success of a museum is the creation of ideal atmospheric conditions. Here the exhibits are as delicate as ancient Egyptian remains. The thermal mass of the concrete roof smooths out extremes of temperature and obviates the need for air conditioning and heating. (Because so much at Duxford is outside, it was felt that the public would accept winter temperatures more akin to those of a hangar than those of a museum building.) A straightforward dehumidifying system does the rest of the job, maintaining the relative humidity at levels well below the 65 per cent figure at which aluminium deteriorates. Filters in the main south-east-facing glazed elevation prevent discoloration of metals and canvas.

But this is no static museum, and the design actively reflects that fact. Through the glazed façade visitors can watch the movement, take-off, flight and landing of many of the collection's historic aircraft. The building was designed to provide a neutral backdrop to the exhibits: simple in form, a half-ellipse in plan, with an emphasis on clarity and natural light. The roof, which uses precast-concrete panels, was developed with Ove Arup. Its single span is the largest of its kind in Europe; its apparent simplicity belies the effort involved. The stresses created by aircraft being hung from the roof mean that a thick shell is required, one that is also double curved, that is, in which the radii change constantly in two directions. Arup has come up with just six concrete components to achieve this, instead of the dozens that might have been expected, given that there are 924 panels in all. The roof is also double-skinned, with the inner layer made up of 274 inverted T-beams, the outer shell of 650 flat panels.

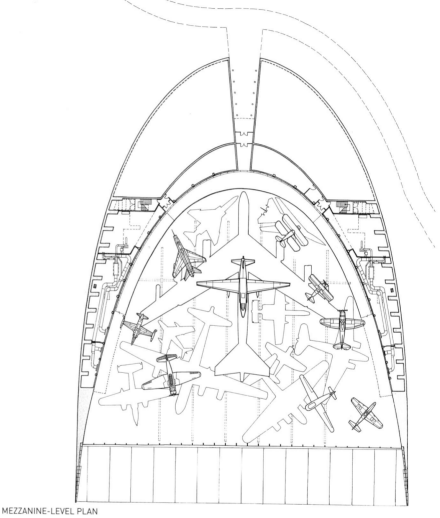

MEZZANINE-LEVEL PLAN

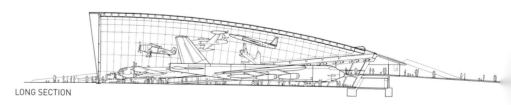

LONG SECTION

PAGES 56–57 The fully glazed façade allows visitors to watch the movement of the museum's non-static exhibits.

TOP AND OPPOSITE From the outside, the building resembles the work of a high-tech mole; inside it is a centimetre-perfect fit for the aircraft it was made to house, not least the B-52 with its 61-metre wingspan.

CLIENT Imperial War Museum STRUCTURAL ENGINEER Ove Arup & Partners CONTRACTOR John Sisk & Son CONTRACT VALUE £7.95 million PHOTOGRAPHER Nigel Young – Foster and Partners

The success of the project lies in the resonance between the elegant engineered form of the building and the technically driven shapes of the aeroplanes that it contains. The building itself sustains the fascination of these objects, reassembling them and presenting them back to the visitor with dramatic intensity. Taking its inspiration from a range of building forms associated with war, from the humble Anderson shelter to hard high-explosive-proof aircraft hangars, the building rises smoothly out of the ground to make a big window on to the airfield. The gesture has an appropriately grand scale that befits the huge space that it faces. Internally, the severely reduced detail of construction gives the building its vast scale. On entering, the aeroplanes are seen against the backdrop of the airfield, as if only in temporary shelter and therefore with a greater sense of realism than is usual for a museum. Most of the aeroplanes stand on the concrete floor level with the runway beyond and are enjoyably accessible. Standing among the aircraft, one is hardly aware of the building.

The museum is a very special building and yet, unusually perhaps for Foster, almost self-effacing. It has a quality beyond that of simply being a museum; it is a memorial to the American air force in World War II. The concrete roof structure conveys a feeling of compression that emphasizes the power of a simple idea.

THE BRITISH LIBRARY
.LONDON NW1 .COLIN ST JOHN WILSON & PARTNERS

Although this project was overlooked for an RIBA Civic and Community Architecture Award, the judges agreed to consider it for the Stirling Prize in view of the immensity of its achievement. The brief was "to provide a self-contained building – which offers an acceptable solution for an indefinite period – for a major part of the reference and information services function of the British Library". Planning constraints meant that the building height could not exceed that of the ridge of St Pancras train-shed next door; similar constraints meant that the main façade had to be set back 75 metres from Euston Road. Other objectives included making the book stock quickly available to as wide a public as possible in an efficient, controlled and pollution-free environment.

This enormous project was initiated in 1975, approved in 1978, and was fourteen years in construction. Inevitably, a twenty-year-old design poses challenges, but in the context of a projected life for such a building of between 200 and 250 years, these are not so great as might be anticipated.

A courtyard facing Euston Road is layered towards the entrance. The vast foyer is an extension of this space, rising gracefully between the top-lit Humanities Reading Room and the side-lit linear Science and Technology Reading Room. Between them, the black glass obelisk of the King's Library lies at the fulcrum of the foyer, beyond which the internal and external terraces of other accommodation rise. The materials are of the highest quality: red brick, powder-coated aluminium and Welsh slate externally; travertine, Portland stone, American oak, maple, bronze, brass and leather inside.

The British Library represents unbroken quality, from the consideration of space to the detailing. It is an architecture of authenticity and permanence within which technology is harnessed but is not expressive. It is a building of immense size and importance, yet it has intimacy and a human quality. It is a building of complexity, yet the programme is clearly legible and provides an unambiguous understanding of circulation and orientation. The architects have demonstrated ingenuity in making the monumental human. This is best seen in the great entrance hall, where the huge volume is broken down by the use of contrasting materials; where there is always a bench to sit on, a balcony to lean on, a piece of art to examine; where stairs are broken into short flights. This is a building in which the success is in the detail: every last reader chair and book trolley has been specially designed. Here the user is in the hands of a master architect, as in an Aalto building. The reference does not flatter the architect whose life-work this is. In a way, this is architecture of the same generation as that of Stirling, and Wilson describes himself as belonging to this alternative tradition of Modernism.

RIGHT This cathedral to learning shares with its religious equivalents a sense of monumental permanence and quality.

OPPOSITE Everything about the library is bespoke: chairs, tables, even book trolleys.

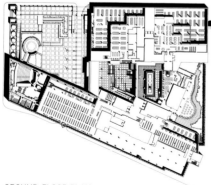

GROUND-FLOOR PLAN

CLIENT The Board of the British Library STRUCTURAL ENGINEER Ove Arup & Partners
CONTRACTORS Laing Management (Phase 1a)/McAlpine Haden Joint Venture
(completion) CONTRACT VALUE £511 million PHOTOGRAPHER John Donat

COMMERZBANK HEADQUARTERS
.FRANKFURT AM MAIN, GERMANY
.FOSTER AND PARTNERS

JOINT WINNER OF THE RIBA COMMERCIAL ARCHITECTURE AWARD

At just under 300 metres and with sixty floors in all, at the time of completion this was the tallest building in Europe and said to be the world's tallest ecological high-rise tower. An outer glass skin allows inner windows to be opened. The plan is triangular, with nine hanging gardens – three on each aspect – overlooking the atrium, switching around the three internal glazed façades as the building rises a dizzying fifty storeys. The raised ground floor, reached on two sides by impressive flights of steps, divides in two. One part allows the public into the otherwise private spaces of the bank with an elegantly designed (by other hands) foodcourt-style restaurant. The other part is given over to a vast corporate foyer, humanized by bronze statues of the people of Frankfurt going about their daily business.

The winter gardens, each with planting that matches its orientation (east, Asian; south, Mediterranean; west, North American), are green oases used by workers for breaks while also providing the building with lungs. They share their views with the inner offices, which, like all the other offices in the building, have opening windows. The atrium and the small floorplans – an aspect of enlightened German planning policy – mean that all the offices are light and airy. Cheerful use of colour helps with orientation.

The natural-ventilation strategy subdivides the tower into four twelve-storey units or 'villages' with four-storey-high central atria and spiralling sky gardens rotating through 120 degrees. Gardens and atria are interlinked for greater natural-ventilation efficiency. Each 'village' is independently controlled by its own weather station. Offices are primarily naturally ventilated, with top-up cooling and mechanical ventilation available. In mechanical-ventilation mode, air is extracted via a glazed cavity to reduce solar gain.

The triangular plan is a satisfying piece of design, giving each façade a favourable aspect and creating a sense of intimacy in the atrium despite the huge scale. The gardens are a *tour de force* that firmly places the building among the most significant modern office towers.

As a big green energy-conscious giant and as a place to work, the Commerzbank is an admirable achievement that sets new standards for office buildings. To be able to open the windows on the fiftieth floor is no small thing. Skyscrapers are seldom contextual, unless they are in Manhattan or Croydon. But this one relates to the ground and its urban context in an easy and unforced way, matching the urban scale with a ring of four-storey buildings. At street level it is generally well-mannered and unusually respectful of its neighbours. The humane ambitions of this building are atypical for a commercial skyscraper.

ABOVE The Commerzbank represents a significant stage in Norman Foster's ongoing search for the humane, intelligent skyscraper.

OPPOSITE The triangular plan works well, not least on the ground floor, producing two wings, one a public space and café (top), the other the corporate foyer, linked by a garden (far right).

CLIENT Immobilienvermietungsgesellschaften Alpha + Beta STRUCTURAL ENGINEERS Ove Arup & Partners with Krebs und Kiefer CONTRACTOR Hochtief CONTRACT VALUE DM525 million PHOTOGRAPHERS Ian Lambot (above)/Nigel Young – Foster and Partners (opposite)

TYPICAL FLOOR PLAN

CRYSTAL PALACE CONCERT PLATFORM .CRYSTAL PALACE PARK, LONDON SE26 .IAN RITCHIE ARCHITECTS
JOINT WINNER OF THE RIBA SPORT AND LEISURE AWARD

The platform is located in Crystal Palace Park, laid out by Joseph Paxton in 1864 to accommodate the Crystal Palace, which was originally created for the Great Exhibition of 1851. The competition-winning scheme involved the design of a permanent outdoor concert platform with support facilities for an eighty-piece orchestra and chorus for major events, as well as for jazz, theatre and use by local clubs and schools. It was part-funded by the Arts Council Lottery, Bromley Council and the government's Single Regeneration Budget (SRB) fund.

The concept was developed from an understanding and recognition of the primary importance of the Paxton landscape. The architects concluded that a simple structure was appropriate to this already complex environment. Two speaker towers, each 9 metres high, containing forty-six speakers, stand as monoliths forward of the stage, which is reached by a drawbridge across a lake. The outside surface is made of Corten A, a steel that protects itself naturally by oxidization, developing a reddish-brown coating. The stage is natural oak, which turns silver. The industrial aesthetic is continued into the backstage areas concealed in the deep steel wedge to the rear.

The concert platform is used seasonally and irregularly, so it stands idle in a public park most of the time. It must therefore have an architectural presence independent of its principal function and be robust and secure. The architects have solved this problem through a combination of pure sculpture and technical ingenuity. On its own, the simplicity of the form in the landscape is dramatic and a credit to the courage of both the architects and their client. When the platform is in use, concealed doors drop down like drawbridges, flaps open to reveal lighting, and the structure is transformed in moments. The innovative acoustics – the world's first outdoor active acoustic system controlled by computer – transmit the sound across the shallow grass bowl that acts as the auditorium for audiences of up to 8000 people.

This building combines artistry with practicality to provide a cost-effective means of maintaining the park's public performances while adding to the quality of its surroundings. The architectural patronage of the local authority has not only ensured the continuation of public performances, but has given the borough a work of art.

ABOVE Ian Ritchie's striking Corten steel concert platform has given Crystal Palace a second landmark.

OPPOSITE This is a piece of working sculpture, transforming itself in moments from artwork to concert platform.

CLIENT London Borough of Bromley **STRUCTURAL ENGINEER** Atelier One
CONTRACTOR Ballast Wiltshier **CONTRACT VALUE** £830,000 **PHOTOGRAPHER** Jocelyne van den Bossche

SITE PLAN

KAISTRASSE OFFICE BUILDING
.DÜSSELDORF, GERMANY .DAVID CHIPPERFIELD ARCHITECTS
WITH INGENHOVEN, OVERDIEK, KAHLEN UND PARTNER
JOINT WINNER OF THE RIBA COMMERCIAL ARCHITECTURE AWARD

This building for 'creative talents' stands in a former industrial area and has a harbourside setting; one of the cranes has been retained as a marker of the site's history. The building is in three parts (two of which are by other architects): two tower-block 'bookends', the Chipperfield one a muscular concrete box, the other a Gehry piece, with the 'books' an office building with larger open-plan floorplates providing two floors of office space by and for the German associate architects for the whole scheme. The Chipperfield building is conceived as a series of double-height lofts with mezzanine floors providing workspaces and exhibition areas for sculptors and painters.

The three elements are modulated and related with extreme care and sophistication as a studied and precise composition of some of the great themes of twentieth-century architecture – from the fineness of Miesian order to the coarseness of Corbusian raw concrete.

The rawness of the building's materials, silhouette and setting all complement one another. The building sits alongside the river, a crane perfectly framed by its overhang. Unlike those that remain in London's Docklands, this is no prop; it stands there squarely on its rails looking like it still means business. But this is no grim warehouse; inside is all light and glowing wood. Chipperfield's is much the best of the three buildings here. Even in the rain, which so often does little for concrete, it looks the part. The ground floor is given over to a restaurant, the windows of which overlook a newly created square: a clever little piece of urban design in an area that appears to have sold its industrial heritage all too willingly for a mess of commercial development. This building echoes its past without mimicking it. A part-glazed lift whisks you effortlessly to the uppermost storeys. Here in the gallery – as in the restaurant – cool raw battened concrete is offset by the warm glow of red teak that suddenly looks fashionable once more (no longer suitable only for stereograms and televisions).

The power of the building is compelling, and its literal but artful transposition of the massing of the older harbour buildings is convincing as a way of making the new do justice to the historic city.

ABOVE Düsseldorf's architectural zoo, from left to right: Gehry; Ingenhoven, Overdiek, Kahlen; Chipperfield.

OPPOSITE David Chipperfield's muscular tower is entirely appropriate to its harbourside setting, but it echoes its industrial past without mimicking it.

CLIENT GbR Kaistrasse STRUCTURAL ENGINEER Arup GmbH CONTRACTOR Strabag Bau
CONTRACT VALUE £3 million PHOTOGRAPHER Julia Oppermann

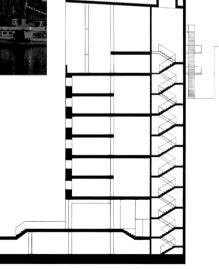

SECTION

LANDESGIROKASSE BANK CENTRAL ADMINISTRATION BUILDING .STUTTGART, GERMANY .BEHNISCH, BEHNISCH & PARTNER

JOINT WINNER OF THE RIBA COMMERCIAL ARCHITECTURE AWARD

This new bank headquarters occupies a whole city block in the centre of Stuttgart, on the rim of a natural bowl in which the city rests. The building's rectangular perimeter encloses a central courtyard, a large part of which is covered by a sloping glass roof, forming an interior hall. The sloping pavement flows uninterrupted into the building. A large area of water, over a bed of cobbles, penetrates the hall, further blurring the edges between interior and exterior and reflecting sunlight inwards. Pivoting mirrors on the roof similarly introduce reflected light into the few darker corners of the building. Cafés, shops and cinemas complement the volume of the courtyard, which has the cheerful atmosphere of a small, busy city square. The mass of the building is humanized, avoiding the appearance of a large city block. The building is naturally ventilated, and solar gain is controlled by automatic external blinds and internal manually operated wooden louvred screens. The asymmetrical corridors are spacious and mostly naturally lit.

It is an exciting and sensorily stimulating building, bursting with energy and packed with invention and wit at every turn. There is playfulness without frivolity. This is a building that is fun but by no means mannered, making an interesting comparison with the nearby Staatsgalerie, the modern building for which the city is most famous. Most importantly, it redefines how a bank headquarters might relate to its employees, its visitors, the passers-by and the city.

To create a bank headquarters that has the air of being as much playground as workplace is no mean achievement. Here are all the Behnisch hallmarks: the use of water and of tilted and intersecting glass planes, both with their hall-of-mirrors capacities; the breaking-down of the boundaries between inside and out by means of the water, glass and vegetation; the intricate deployment of natural ventilation and sunshading; and of course colour. The colours are striking without being brash; they look as if they are made to withstand the weather. They are also integral to the building rather than being retrospectively applied for effect. This is perhaps because the architect collaborated, as is his wont, at an early stage with his artistic partner, Christian Kandzia (who also takes his photographs). Colour is at work inside as well as out, making this a lively and stimulating place in which to work.

BELOW LEFT As with the Staatsgalerie, Stuttgart's planners have wisely insisted that major buildings should contribute to the city by bringing the building line on to the street.

BELOW RIGHT AND OPPOSITE Banking can be fun: Behnisch's inside-out building is as much playground as workplace.

CLIENT Landesgirokasse STRUCTURAL ENGINEER Leonhardt, Andrä und Partner CONSTRUCTION MANAGEMENT BB&P with Hans-Joachim Maile CONTRACT VALUE DM2 million PHOTOGRAPHER Christian Kandzia

GROUND-FLOOR PLAN

PRIVATE HOUSE IN HAMPSTEAD
.LONDON NW3
.RICK MATHER ARCHITECTS
WINNER OF THE RIBA HOUSES AND HOUSING AWARD

This extraordinary house, filled with light and the distorting refractions of water and reflections of glass, results from an ambitious brief that called for a family house with pool and roof terrace to be built on a site with existing planning permission for two semi-detached pastiche-Georgian houses. The job was won in competition with three other firms. Extensive negotiations took place with a number of local conservation and amenity groups, with English Heritage and the Royal Fine Art Commission, and with planners and local residents before work began.

A solid concrete-frame structure was chosen to deal with the large voids in the floors. It is possible to lie in the basement pool and look up through the glass ceiling to the double-height living space and through a further roof light to the rooms above. A glass slot runs from the basement to the first floor on the rear façade, with part of the ground floor suspended via a steel column from a concrete rig beam at roof level. Structural glass is used extensively through the house, and for the balustrading to the roof gardens and for the stairs. Materials used in the non-glass floors include stressed plywood, part-stressed concrete and timber joists. Externally, the architect has used brick, reconstituted stone and a polymer render on stainless steel lath. An elastomeric spray-applied paint accommodates movement and provides a very even finish over the house.

The house has a mechanical ventilation system supplying fresh air to all rooms. A boiler in the basement provides heating and hot water for the house, pool and adjacent steam and shower room. There is a heat-recovery unit in the roof, linked to ducts and grilles throughout the house. A rainwater-storage tank in the garden also serves the roof terraces.

The house brings together Rick Mather's understanding of and commitment to the classic Modern Movement style and his highly developed use of glass. The interior is a dramatic exploration of Cubist interpenetration of spaces in which the glass plane – whether vertical or horizontal – adds an element of newness and surprise. All the details of domestic life are discreetly taken care of, with beautifully detailed cupboards, sliding doors, and bathroom and kitchen interiors. There are terraces for all the bedrooms and a roof terrace above with an exceptional view across Hampstead. Both internally and externally there is a skilful manipulation of light and view, while privacy is maintained in relation to the surrounding buildings.

The clients – a married couple – are both pleased with the house, even though they have different levels of commitment to a 'minimal' lifestyle. The house is used a lot for entertaining, and it is obvious that its drama is very suitable for the purpose.

ABOVE The front elevation is suggestive of deco styling, but this is a fiercely contemporary house.

OPPOSITE The crispness of the rear elevation is more reflective of the interiors, where the detailing would be appropriate to the most generously endowed art gallery.

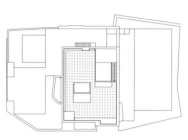

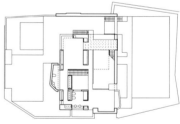

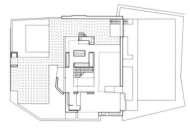

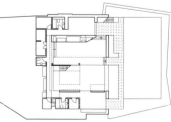

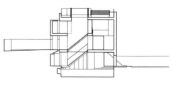

FLOOR PLANS AND SECTION

CLIENT Private STRUCTURAL ENGINEER Atelier One CONTRACTOR Hosier & Dickinson
CONTRACT VALUE £750,000 PHOTOGRAPHER Richard Bryant – Arcaid

70

QUAY BAR
.MANCHESTER .STEPHENSON/BELL
JOINT WINNER OF THE RIBA SPORT AND LEISURE AWARD

The client is the Wolverhampton & Dudley Breweries, or Banks's, which has wholeheartedly embraced the trend towards a café-bar culture in Liverpool and Manchester. The brief was to create good contemporary architecture that responds to its programme and its context. Because the site is 4.5 metres below road level, the two apartments required by the brief are stacked one upon the other in an exaggerated way above the bar. This allows the building to advertise its presence to the whole of the Castlefield Basin, where it is extremely prominent. At the same time, at canal level it stretches out towards the tranquility of the water. The building reflects the multilayered nature of the site by allowing access at all levels, from the canalside or from the busy road.

Robust materials reflect the heritage of the site, from Roman fort to coal and slag depository. The horizontal expression of the curtain walling facing the canal contrasts vigorously with the vertical emphasis of the standing-seamed stainless steel stair tower, which soars above and behind the expanse of the steel roof, and the creamy softness of the rendered apartment tower. Original works of art for the bar were commissioned at an early stage by the architects, who persuaded the brewery to redeploy its 'bric-a-brac' fund for the purpose.

In essence this is a large single-volume pub that rises far beyond the dreary norm for this building type. The building makes the most of its site on a rejuvenated canal basin. Two-storey glazing overlooking the water provides excellent views along with admirable levels of daylight. The raised timber decking on the waterfront is neatly done, and the disabled access is elegantly incorporated. The materials used in the bars – heavy timber, polished concrete floor and stainless steel – are tough but appropriate and in no way overwhelming. A mezzanine level serving pub grub benefits from views across the canal while linking to the higher level road behind the building. Given that the building is largely below this level, the architects did well to give it a clear presence on the road with the two-storey landlord's flat and a prominent illuminated feature that creates a local landmark.

This is an exceptionally ambitious building for a brewery to commission. It is a welcome addition to the few modern pubs that break the mould of decades of old-world pastiche.

ABOVE AND RIGHT A rarity in the 1990s – a well-designed pub. It was also one of the key regenerators of the Castlefield area of Manchester.

OPPOSITE The balustraded glass bridge draws people in from the street.

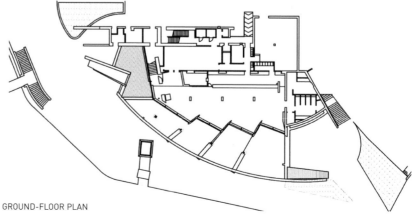

GROUND-FLOOR PLAN

CLIENT Wolverhampton & Dudley Breweries **STRUCTURAL ENGINEER** Peter Taylor & Associates **CONTRACTOR** Roland Bardsley **CONTRACT VALUE** £1.25 million **PHOTOGRAPHER** David Grandorge

RICHARD ATTENBOROUGH CENTRE FOR DISABILITY AND THE ARTS, UNIVERSITY OF LEICESTER. LEICESTER
.IAN TAYLOR WITH BENNETTS ASSOCIATES

WINNER OF THE RIBA EDUCATION AND HEALTH AWARD (SPONSORED BY THE DEPARTMENT OF HEALTH)

The Richard Attenborough Centre was one of the first recipients of Lottery funding – to the tune of £730,000. Lord Attenborough gave his name and clout to the fund-raising effort, and the new building was opened by the Princess of Wales in 1997, in what turned out to be one of her last public engagements.

The centre was the subject of a two-part competition funded by *The Independent* and organized by the RIBA, leading to the appointment of the complete design team, including structural, service, acoustics and cost consultants, in 1994. The funding has been used to create an arts centre that places the needs of people with a wide range of disabilities at the heart of the design process. The result is a building that avoids knee-jerk solutions in the shape of the disability aids that can offend the very people whose needs they seek to serve. The centre is about access in all senses of the word. It is open to all with disabilities, providing courses that range from arts access to higher degrees. But it is also about providing access to other people who previously had difficulty getting on to arts courses. It encourages participation and performance to a professional standard. It is a truly open building.

The structure employs a variety of construction techniques to respond to the character of the three parts of the building. At the rear a closed brick box provides a galleries hall, flanked at ground level by the music and drama rooms, which open on to tight-walled yards. This is linked by a narrow top-lit glass void to a front half that is a more open concrete and steel-framed block. This hall provides the foyer space and it sits under a cedar-clad upper storey containing the sculpture studio and research library. This organizational clarity and simple circulation pattern are fundamental to users with a variety of abilities finding their way around. The building's readability is reinforced by marked changes in light levels, textures and acoustics. This is a building designed to appeal to a majority of the senses: sight, sound, touch and – with an aromatic cedar-clad main hall – smell.

This is not a big statement building. Its attraction is more subtle and lies in the high levels of ingenuity, care and insight that clearly ran through the whole design process. It is a thoughtful and considered response to a specific set of needs and a difficult context. It is a testament to the unfashionable view that good architecture need not be sensational architecture.

The centre's director, Dr Eleanor Hartley, said, "We wanted to get away from the idea of a building with loads of flashy add-on ramps and bright multicoloured furniture that shouted disability. Instead we went for a design that was less patronizingly accessible and far more in keeping with what people with disabilities actually said they wanted."

ABOVE This was one of the first buildings to place the needs of disabled people at the heart of the design process. Much of what it does has since been enshrined in legislation.

OPPOSITE The internal spaces are all about the senses: sight, sound, touch, even – with the use of cedar – smell.

CLIENT Simon Britton, Director of Estates, University of Leicester **STRUCTURAL ENGINEER** Curtins Consulting Engineers **CONTRACTOR** John Laing Construction **CONTRACT VALUE** £1.15 million **PHOTOGRAPHER** Peter Cook – VIEW

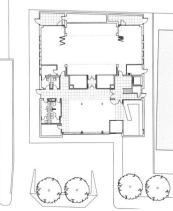

GROUND-FLOOR PLAN

ST BENNO CATHOLIC GRAMMAR SCHOOL
.DRESDEN, GERMANY
.BEHNISCH, BEHNISCH & PARTNER
WINNER OF THE RIBA ARCHITECTURE IN EDUCATION AWARD

The rebirth of the St Benno Catholic Grammar School in the centre of Dresden is symbolic of the birth of the new Germany. Shut down by the Nazis, the school remained closed under Communism, its religious ethos being antipathetic to both regimes. It is surrounded by five six-storey housing blocks, built to replace housing destroyed by blanket bombing of the city by the Allies in World War II.

The school, the winning entry in a 1992 competition, was built between 1994 and 1996. It is located between the city's ring road and the terraced banks of the Elbe River. The conflict between aggression and tranquility provided a basis for the design. The site is long and terminates in a public square. The blue wall of the street façade screens the interior space and provides it with a calming buffer against the hostility of the traffic. The western façade opens up to a colourful interior garden, similar in mood to the vineyards and terraces of the Elbe.

The design of the school is intended to help the children develop personality and character (neither trait much in demand perhaps in the Communist era). The classrooms are divided into three blocks of four on the two upper storeys, each differently orientated so as to create terraces on first- and second-floor levels. The device also obviates the need for traditional long, straight school corridors. The entrance is at two levels. A foyer rises through all four floors, lit by a large window and by a glass roof. The library, mediathèque and performance space – with retractable walls – lead off the first floor. On the ground floor the cafeteria, separated from a courtyard by a glass wall, overlooks a basement gym, itself lit by high windows.

What on first sight seem arbitrary devices – the jangled façade elements, the asymmetrical corridors, the sudden changes in roof level – work surprisingly in harmony to produce a rich range of spaces and functions, all apparently effortlessly strung along the line dictated by the site. The use of colour is bold and confident. Teachers seemed very pleased with the building, and there is a waiting list of applicants. Behnisch's sophisticated architecture is surprisingly appropriate to a school – more so perhaps than to the more rigid orthodoxies demanded by corporate clients. The bravura is almost childlike in its creativity; perhaps that is why the kids enjoy this school so much.

There is very little to find fault with in this building, which seems to have accomplished everything it set out to do without over-reaching itself. It provides richness and complexity without becoming gratuitously complex or mannered.

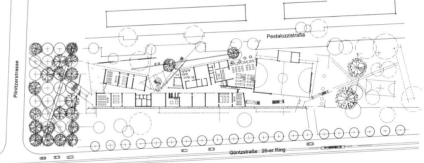

GROUND-FLOOR PLAN

TOP The school, with its fragmented façade, mediates between the street and the hill behind.

OPPOSITE Behnisch's extraordinary, playful architecture is even more suited to a school than it is to a commercial office; that's why the children enjoy it so much.

CLIENT Bishop's Diocese of Dresden **STRUCTURAL ENGINEER** Fritz Wenzel
CONSTRUCTION MANAGEMENT BB&P **CONTRACT VALUE** DM49.5 million
PHOTOGRAPHER Christian Kandzia

TEMPLE OF CONCORD AND VICTORY, STOWE LANDSCAPE GARDENS
.BUCKINGHAM, BUCKINGHAMSHIRE
.PETER INSKIP & PETER JENKINS ARCHITECTS
WINNER OF THE RIBA CONSERVATION AWARD

One of the most important Neo-classical buildings in Europe, the temple was begun in 1747, when it was known as the Grecian Building. Over the next 250 years it was altered many times. A conservation plan was crucial. This assesses the cultural significance of a place, identifies where that significance is vulnerable, and defines policies for its future management. The plan indicated that the building should be returned to its form at the end of the eighteenth century. As the project was linked with an enabling works contract, the risk of surprises always associated with historic buildings was reduced, and the work came in under budget.

The statue of Victory was restored and the tympanum sculptures were conserved. The renders on the pediments and entablature were conserved, with missing sections replaced. Sixteen Ionic columns removed in the nineteenth century to build a chapel were surveyed so that their replacements matched exactly. These were turned by computer-controlled lathes, then hand-finished *in situ*. The plinth was repaired and strengthened with a grid of stainless steel rods in epoxy resin. Archaeological investigation revealed the ghostings of inscriptions removed from the medallions in the nineteenth century, so they could be reinstated. Similar meticulous studies made possible reconstruction of the aedicule, removed in 1845.

Conventional scrapes rarely document the full paint history of a building, so microscopic paint analysis was used to identify the eighteenth-century finishes. As a result, the doors were painted Prussian blue, the gilding was matched accurately, and the renders, plasters and stone were limewashed, giving a unity and lightness to the building that had been completely lost.

Finally, much work has been done on the temple's setting. The planting has been pulled back so the building can be seen clearly at the head of the valley. Cedars planted by Queen Victoria will not be replaced when they die. The work has revealed the foundations of groups of Classical statues: Hercules and Antaeus, Hercules and the Philistines and the Dancing Faun. These have been restored, putting the Temple of Concord and Victory back into its original magnificent Arcadian setting.

It is good to see knowledgeable and professional expertise applied to this successful restoration. It enhances greatly its surroundings and delights visitors. The temple has been beautifully renovated but not over-restored. Although in effect no more than a garden folly, albeit on a grand scale, the building is historically important. The work done to put it back to its original form has been carried out in a way entirely consistent with its role as a set piece in one of the great eighteenth-century Romantic landscapes.

ABOVE Inskip & Jenkins applied state-of-the-art computer techniques and materials to the conservation and restoration of this grand eighteenth-century folly.

OPPOSITE Sixteen of the Ionic columns removed in the nineteenth century to build a chapel were measured *in situ* so that their replacements matched exactly.

CLIENT National Trust for Places of Historic Interest or Natural Beauty
STRUCTURAL ENGINEER Ralph Mills Associates **CONTRACTOR** Linford-Bridgeman
CONTRACT VALUE £1.5 million **PHOTOGRAPHER** Inskip & Jenkins

AXONOMETRIC

THE STIRLING PRIZE 1998
.TOM DYCKHOFF

ARCHITECTURE CRITIC OF *THE TIMES*

Ah, life before the icon. Do you remember it? Before blobs and shards and funny angles? Before Libeskind and Hadid, when we were just, only just, hearing about Frank Gehry's strange beast in Bilbao? Deconstructivism may have been invented in the 1970s and 1980s, but British architecture in 1998 was still dressed in few cheeky angles, sexy curves or fancy colours. For the moment, all we needed to keep ourselves architecturally amused were wood floors, acres of space and light, structural-glass balustrades and a whole heap of brushed steel. Simpler times.

In 1998 we were one still-euphoric year into a Labour government. But, in architecture at least, we were dancing to the tune left by the previous, somewhat greyer administration. Not that John Major's government was bad news for buildings – far from it. It's often forgotten that it was Major who instigated the National Lottery, in 1994 – one of the biggest injections of public money into major building works for well over a decade, the first sizable fruits of which were finally beginning to show in the RIBA Awards. The 1998 awards showed a country at last finding its architectural confidence again after more than two decades in the Post-modern doldrums. We can argue about who or what to blame for the doldrums until the cows come home – the oil crisis, the retraction of the welfare state, Thatcherism, the anti-Modernist agenda, Prince Charles – but it certainly made Britain a rather architecturally conservative (aka boring) place when I was growing up in the 1980s.

Now all that was gone. Britain had rediscovered its passion for contemporary design. Loft living, *Wallpaper** magazine, IKEA chucking out the chintz all played their part in championing modern taste at home, as did the slow economic recovery from the recession of the early 1990s, loosening our, and developers', grip on the purse strings. But it was the Lottery-funded building programme that led the way. At last we were building again, building a nation of loft-livers, with every last hamlet doing a Barcelona, putting on a show to grab the attention of investors and consumers. Designer shops and visitor centres were now the order of the day, coffee bars, museums, art galleries, shopping malls, and, coming here one day soon, architectural icons, all designed to give us something 'creative' to do while keeping the consumerist economy's coffers frisky. It was as if all those Modernist architects – Foster, Grimshaw, Rogers and their contemporaries – who had been banished from building in their native land for fifteen years were let loose at last. The old order hath crumbled. Nostalgia is no more. Modernism has triumphed in Blighty! Seventy years late, mind, but we're a cautious bunch.

Politics is quick, but architecture takes a long time. When the first monuments to this new nation were being completed, along comes Tony Blair to claim the spoils. Cool Britannia was set against this loft-living, Conran-styled Modernist landscape, just like the one inside Le Pont de la Tour, the swanky Thames-side restaurant where the Blairs wined and dined the Clintons for the cameras. Glass, brushed steel and wood floors became Britain's new vernacular. Cool Britannia indeed, cool and (whisper it) ever so slightly passionless.

Still, most of us were jolly grateful to have contemporary architecture of any scale or quality for the first time in years. And 1998's Stirling shortlist definitely screamed quality. True, four of the buildings were still abroad, an echo from the 1980s, when newspaper articles would bemoan our architects getting more work in Europe than at home. David Chipperfield's Kaistrasse office in Düsseldorf is nice, elegant, true to the new neo-Modernist agenda, but not a building, alas, to set the pulses racing.

Norman Foster's Frankfurt Commerzbank updated his quest for the intelligent, humane skyscraper that began with the Hongkong and Shanghai Bank headquarters and led to the Gherkin, but, aesthetically, didn't refine it. There was an exhilarating blast from the future of funny angles with Behnisch's St Benno Catholic Grammar School, Dresden, and Landesgirokasse bank building, Stuttgart, although the angles were still pretty low resolution.

There was a blast from the past, too, the past before those architectural doldrums set in, when quality, large-scale public architecture hadn't been eradicated by enterprise zones and the Private Finance Initiative. Colin St John Wilson's British Library was a vindication of his 'alternative tradition' of English Modernism, before the baby was thrown out with the bathwater in the 1980s. But its freakish tardiness – in part caused by those very doldrums – perhaps reminded the jury too much of the past at a time when its members were hunting for monuments to the confidence of the present.

The lack of major buildings in Britain meant inclusion on the shortlist of projects that, though perfectly honed, were, in retrospect, minor works. If quality per square centimetre were a Stirling criterion, Ian Ritchie's Crystal Palace concert platform might have won hands down, with its bold, gutsy, sculptural form and use of materials. Ritchie contented himself instead with the first Stephen Lawrence Prize, for his Terrasson Cultural Greenhouse in France. Inskip's and Jenkins's restoration of the Temple of Concord and Victory at Stowe? Nice, accomplished. Ditto Stephenson/Bell's Manchester Quay Bar and Ian Taylor's and Bennetts Associates' Richard Attenborough Centre, Leicester, doubly so considering what they achieved in the fields of pub and accessible design. But while exceptional at the time in setting the standard for good modern, everyday architecture (a standard that, without the doldrums, might have been standard years ago), they were hardly that notch above the norm necessary for a Stirling winner.

No, there were only two clear favourites. As Hugh Pearman put it at the time, the judges split into Fosterites and Matherites, one pressing for the supremacy of float-away high tech, the other for that of weighty, white-cube Modernism, essentially the tradition of either Mies van der Rohe or Le Corbusier. In the end, Rick Mather's neo-Corbusian Hampstead house lost to Norman Foster's American Air Museum, Duxford – what Foster does well, a simple idea, stunningly executed. Both were a celebration of a country getting bolder and bolder, with clients (public and private) willing to experiment, a public keen for architectural thrills, and architects able to deliver. Both, however, revealed a country still playing catch-up after the doldrums, still learning to build, and love, Mies and Corb. If there was life beyond these Modernist masters, it hadn't reached us yet. But it would – next year, in fact.

.JUDGES

Marco Goldschmied RIBA president (chair)
Amanda Baillieu Editor of the *RIBA Journal*
Stella McCartney Fashion designer
Michael Manser Chair of the RIBA Awards Group
Rick Mather Architect and Stirling Prize runner-up in 1998

.THE STIRLING PRIZE WINNER

.THE STIRLING PRIZE SHORTLIST

.THE STIRLING PRIZE 1999

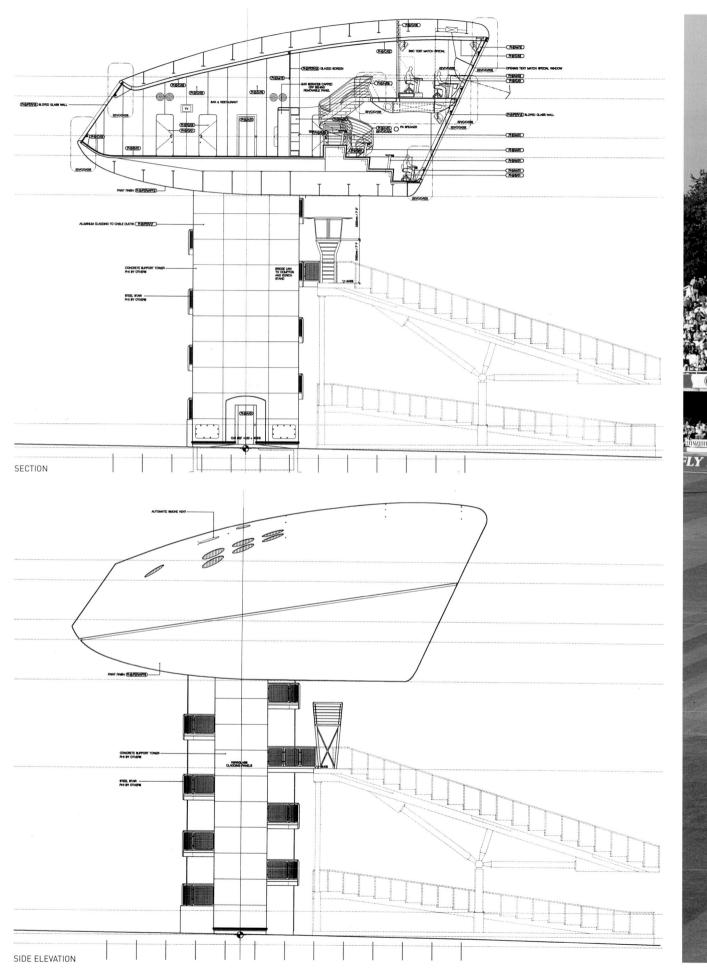

SECTION

SIDE ELEVATION

NATWEST MEDIA CENTRE, LORD'S CRICKET GROUND .LONDON NW8 .FUTURE SYSTEMS

ALSO JOINT WINNER OF THE RIBA ARTS AND LEISURE AWARD

Digital alarm clock, bar-code reader, alien starship: these are a few of the press's attempts to convey an impression of a structure that might indeed seem alien to its very conventional setting. But this is Lord's and Lord's is different from any other cricket ground. The Media Centre is an accepted part of the summer scene.

This is one instance in which reality has caught up with fiction. An Archigram Walking City pod has marched into Lord's – or rather been borne here on the back of a lorry – and taken up residence. It is perhaps the best example in this country of 'technology transfer' – the transposition of the methods of one industry (or, in this case, several: boat-building, and car and aeroplane manufacture) to another. It happened at the end of both world wars: in 1918 aircraft production lines were turned over to the production of cars, and in 1945 similar factories were converted to make prefabs. But those initiatives petered out.

Future Systems – which is very much in the Archigram tradition – recognized the 'eternal and sacred' atmosphere of the ground in its competition entry, yet it came up with a structure that is entirely new. As a media centre, it is both the medium and the message. Its soft lines, not least in its less-photographed back, reflect both its origins in a Cornish boatyard and the sweeping curves of the stands. It is the world's first all-aluminium semi-monocoque building, using the technique of welding the skin on to a structure of ribs and spars characteristic of boat- and aircraft-building, obviating the need for obstructive columns. Internally, it is as comfortable and luxurious as a 1950s Chevrolet, the baby-blue upholstery of which inspired it. It hovers 15 metres above the ground, providing perfect all-round views for journalists and allowing access underneath to the Nursery Ground beyond. It addresses the Victorian pavilion opposite, speaking as volubly of the end of one century as the older building does of the previous one. It also faces due west, hence the need for comfort cooling, partly in the form of the kind of individual plastic nozzles used to cool the fevered brows of travellers aboard passenger jets. During test matches 240 journalists sit in serried ranks on white Arne Jacobsen chairs at white computer desks. They can use electrically operated blinds when, towards close of play, the sun is low. External glare, which has been known to stop cricket matches elsewhere, is avoided here as the window can be tilted through 25 degrees.

The NatWest Media Centre became an instant icon, a large white eye on the world of cricket communicating the MCC's belief in the future of the game and contrasting almost irreverently with the traditional pavilion it faces. The simple design clearly communicates its purpose and imposes itself on this historic arena, thus avoiding the risk of becoming just another charm on the Lord's bracelet. The structure suggests a new world

of off-site manufacturing and a level of consistent quality that (sadly) is more associated with the car industry than with construction. One of the most impressive aspects of the design is the way it neatly avoids the age-old problems of scale, mass and context, which traditional forms find difficult to transcend. These issues just do not apply to its sleek form. Concern has been expressed about the complexities of maintaining such a building, but then, it is only used for part of the year and can be cleaned before each match, ensuring that it retains its new, crisp white appearance.

The NatWest Media Centre is a TV personality. It is its own thing, completely unusual and totally uncompromising. It is a breath of architectural fresh air. Judges try to put themselves into the position of an eight-year-old when they first see a building, and they all agreed that this was the one in which they would have the most fun as kids.

The Media Centre is a complete one-off: a wacky solution to a singular problem. Future Systems had been wanting to do this for a long time, and there is something brilliant about having a dream and seeing it through. In so many ways this was the building of 1999: an extraordinary iconic structure that landed in the middle of Lord's and changed the face of cricket. It was the twentieth century – in the nick of time. It may or may not be the future, but it certainly works.

PAGES 84–85 The Media Centre has come to be accepted by a conservative sport in a way that a less bold solution might never have been.

BELOW AND OPPOSITE The window is tilted through 25 degrees to stop reflections of a low sun getting in the cricketers' eyes and stopping play.

CLIENT Marylebone Cricket Club STRUCTURAL ENGINEER Ove Arup & Partners
CONTRACTOR Pendennis Shipyard CONTRACT VALUE £5 million
PHOTOGRAPHER Richard Davies

THE MUSEUM OF SCOTLAND
.EDINBURGH .BENSON + FORSYTH
STIRLING PRIZE RUNNER-UP

Although the Museum of Scotland did not receive an Arts and Leisure Category Award, for the second year running the Stirling judges exercised their right to call in a scheme and place it on the list for consideration for the Stirling Prize.

The museum is a public building of enormous significance for the city and the country, not least in that its completion coincided with Scotland's regaining a greater degree of independence than it had had at any time in the past three centuries. Externally, the building makes a strong contemporary statement while remaining rooted in the vernacular of the capital city. The simplicity of its forms – the rectangular exhibition block, the cylindrical tower, the curved cantilevered light-reflecting roof terrace – are all given an urban texture by the stone banding, the slit windows and the bridges that link all the elements.

The museum stands beside the High Victorian confection of the Royal Museum of Scotland and, without seeking to compete, more than matches it in its seriousness and ambition. With its solid drum-tower entrance and soaring internal spaces, this museum takes the Scottish baronial tradition and gives it new and exciting life.

Defined as it is by the façades around it, the building seeks to be rigorously contextual, responding dynamically by reinforcing or subverting the existing street pattern. The tower forms a hinge between the north and west façades, acting as a focal point at the convergence of five routes into the city. The height of the perimeter galleries respects that of the buildings to the north, while elements along Bristo Port reflect the asymmetry of the smaller-scale buildings to the south. Meanwhile, the core gallery rises like a castle keep through the curtain wall.

The deliberate addition of complexity to a fundamentally simple plan, particularly internally, is at times taken to excess. But in the final analysis, the integration of a building of this kind into its urban context and the creation of a new landmark for Edinburgh, a city that already contains much of the physical heritage of Scotland, represent a considerable architectural achievement. In the context of this dramatic city it makes a strong and contemporary statement. The simplicity of the external forms creates an urban impact on this site, generating a series of changing views and glimpses from all around the city. The interior spaces are dramatic and befit a public museum of this importance. The care with which each exhibit has been located and displayed is particularly impressive.

The complexity of the plan and circulation route through the building makes for one of the most enjoyable elements of the museum. All is not revealed and clear; instead, the visitor is made to explore and revisit. In its non-prescriptive way the building therefore stands at one extreme of the spectrum of museum design, at the other end of which is the rigid, predetermined visitor experience that many museum designers insist on.

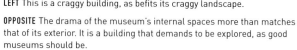

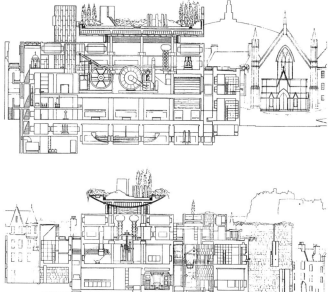

LEFT This is a craggy building, as befits its craggy landscape.

OPPOSITE The drama of the museum's internal spaces more than matches that of its exterior. It is a building that demands to be explored, as good museums should be.

SECTIONS AA AND BB

CLIENT Trustees of the National Museums of Scotland STRUCTURAL ENGINEER Anthony Hunt Associates MANAGEMENT CONTRACTOR Bovis Construction (Scotland) CONTRACT VALUE £44.85 million PHOTOGRAPHER Richard Bryant – Arcaid

NORTH GREENWICH UNDERGROUND STATION
.LONDON SE10 .ALSOP LYALL & STÖRMER WITH JLE PROJECT TEAM
JOINT WINNER OF THE RIBA CIVIC AND COMMUNITY ARCHITECTURE AWARD

The striking North Greenwich station, built to begin the long-term regeneration of the derelict peninsula, immediately acted as the catalyst for the choice of site for the Millennium Dome. By Alsop Lyall & Störmer to construction-tender stage, it was completed over several years by one of Roland Paoletti's Jubilee line extension project teams. The collaboration has produced one of the most efficient, free-spirited and poetic stations on the line. Because of the station's location in what was originally a wilderness site, Paoletti was able to use colour in a way that would not have been allowed elsewhere. The result is spectacular in the scale of its ambition and achievement.

As the station serving the Millennium Dome, North Greenwich was designed to handle 120,000 passengers an hour. The simple hall-like arrangement gives it the spatial clarity of a major public building. From Foster's cool, elegant, white transport interchange, which sits on top, the passenger descends past walls of blue glass, vivid with real cobalt, to a wide deck level suspended in space, with the tracks visible below on either side. More escalators lead down to the platform-level concourse. Here glass doors slide apart as trains arrive and their doors open. The void looks staggering, but the public areas at North Greenwich are no bigger than those at any other Underground station; it is simply the powerful effect of good architecture at work

in opening them up. Ultramarine mosaic tiles clad the V-shaped columns and walls, with a paler blue terrazzo on the floor.

The scale is boldly declared in the open layout of the station, to the extent that an initial visit is almost shocking in its intensity, while being at the same time immensely pleasing. The ambition of the new JLE stations has surely not been seen in London's public transport since Charles Holden's stations in the 1930s. It is worth a trip on the Underground just to see it, but this station brightens the journey of any commuter.

Grand in scale, North Greenwich station is essentially about drama. Although it is famous as the blue station, its power comes from the soaring spaces, changing levels and exposed vertical circulation. Glass side panels allow passengers to look at the platforms below, enhancing the feeling of space. Once down on platform level, they can experience exciting vertiginous views back up to concourse level. The feeling of being in a subterranean cavern – far from being unpleasant – is almost other-worldly, and is enhanced by the use of ultramarine blue on the walls, floors and ceiling. The bigger issue here is that, despite the restrictions imposed by the client, the architect has managed to turn what is normally a humdrum experience (waiting for a Tube train) into something very special.

SECTION FACING NORTH

ABOVE Will Alsop has done it again: thrown good public money but to great effect, and this time in the United Kingdom.

OPPOSITE Alsop's soaring blue spaces provided a fittingly sci-fi end to the twentieth century.

CLIENT London Underground **STRUCTURAL ENGINEER** Benaim Works Joint Venture
CONTRACTORS Sir Robert McAlpine/Wayss & Freytag **CONTRACT VALUE** £110 million
PHOTOGRAPHER Roderick Coyne

RANELAGH MULTIDENOMINATIONAL SCHOOL
.DUBLIN, IRELAND
.O'DONNELL + TUOMEY
WINNER OF THE RIBA EDUCATION AWARD

The agglomeration of buildings forming the old school produced the starting point for the design of the new. The existing ridgeline of the tin church was used as the height limit for the new building, and the line of its north wall set the distance of the new building line from the Georgian terrace behind. The old railings were also preserved and used to enclose a landscaped play area between the school and the terrace. The pitched roofs and first-floor walkway also refer back to the old buildings, but with a distinctly modern spin. The cladding is timber and the roofs are finished in terne-coated steel, which weathers to look like lead. The street elevation is quite different. It is broken into two-storey blocks of paired classrooms with a single-storey link between them, topped by a small roof terrace. These pairs of classrooms and the entry porch are faced with stone taken from an old boundary wall, while reclaimed brick is used for the rest of the main façade and end elevations.

The new building responds to the existing street scale and its wider Georgian context by breaking its street elevation into a series of brick 'houses' while at the back reunifying it with a light wood pergola and loggia.

Considering the initial array of objectors, the design is brave, not least because the architects both had children at the school. (This was the second design; the first, by the education department's own architects, was refused after hostile local reaction.) The exterior perfectly expresses its internal function in a quiet, restrained way. Inside, the spaces are delightful, combining the subtle use of exposed concrete, unpainted timber and painted blockwork. The colour scheme is varied and clearly very successful for a primary school.

FIRST-FLOOR PLAN

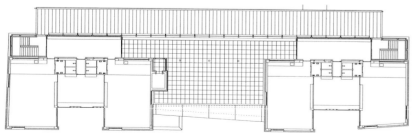

CLIENT Ranelagh Multidenominational School STRUCTURAL ENGINEER Fearon O'Neill Rooney CONTRACTOR Pierce Healy Developments CONTRACT VALUE IR£1.16 million PHOTOGRAPHER Dennis Gilbert – VIEW

ABOVE O'Donnell + Tuomey's subtle architecture makes magic of necessity: here the roofline of a demolished tin church set the height for the new building; stone is reclaimed from a boundary wall.

OPPOSITE Pairs of classrooms give a domestic rhythm to the street elevation and internally they add structure to the educational life of the school.

REICHSTAG, THE NEW GERMAN PARLIAMENT
.BERLIN, GERMANY
.FOSTER AND PARTNERS
WINNER OF THE RIBA CONSERVATION AWARD

Foster and Partners won the open competition to make a home for the new German parliament in the old Reichstag. Although the building was sited in West Berlin, its proximity to the Wall meant that it had been little used since a crude 1960s makeover. The original proposal was to place a canopy, supported by a slender portico, over the whole building. Perhaps this was too irreverent an approach; a new masterplan insisted on the preservation and visibility of the shell. The practice decided instead to make the building a living museum as well as a working parliament and a highly energy-conscious structure. The poor 1960s accretions were removed, revealing the clarity of the original design, opening up interior courtyards and reinstating the ceremonial entrance as a democratic point of entry for politicians and public alike. The same philosophy is repeated throughout, with the public becoming a part of the process: practically, by paying for the building's maintenance through the money spent in the café; symbolically, by means of the elevated viewing platform, reached by helical ramps, from where they look down on their representatives in the chamber below.

Foster's transparent hemisphere replaces Paul Wallot's original decorative dome. The ramps wind around the beehive structure that is a key part of the green strategy of the building, containing energy-supplying photovoltaic cells. This design also reflects daylight into the chamber and is a part of the natural-ventilation system, being used to remove hot air. In all, this is the first major public building to be powered by renewable resources – sunflower or rapeseed oil, which helps reduce carbon dioxide emissions, with solar power providing lighting. Water comes from an artesian well deep below the building, and brown water is collected from the roofs for use in the lavatories.

The judges were impressed by the way in which Foster confronts the sense of history that pervades the building, not least by preserving the graffiti of the Russian soldiers who occupied it in 1945. He exposes the past plainly and simply and in doing so exposes the visitor to the scale of Germany's transformation since the mid-twentieth century. The history of the building is somehow entwined in this new symbol of democracy, and the design subtly balances thoughts of the past with a vision of the future.

The peeling-away of the various layers added in the 1950s and 1960s to obscure the original building has created a unique sense of its endurance, which contrasts strikingly with the limited and controlled use of modern materials and technology. This is perhaps the most impressive thing about the quality of the design. A symbiotic relationship. No tricks. The old and new together in a harmony that celebrates a better future without forgetting the past. In short, it is a building that heralds the rebirth of a nation.

CLIENT Bundesbaugesellschaft Berlin STRUCTURAL ENGINEERS Ove Arup & Partners/Schlaich Bergermann und Partner/Leonhardt, Andrä und Partner CONTRACTOR Büro am Lützowplatz CONTRACT VALUE £265 million PHOTOGRAPHER Nigel Young – Foster and Partners

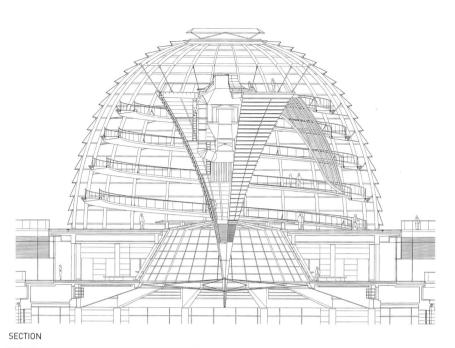

SECTION

ABOVE The juxtaposition of good modern details with the conserved original fabric is what this project is all about.

OPPOSITE Norman Foster has replaced Paul Wallot's dome with a transparent one, winding a ramp around a structure containing many of the building's environmental systems and reflecting and funnelling light into the chamber below.

THE RIVER & ROWING MUSEUM
.MILL MEADOWS, HENLEY-ON-THAMES, OXFORDSHIRE
.DAVID CHIPPERFIELD ARCHITECTS
JOINT WINNER OF THE RIBA ARTS AND LEISURE AWARD

The pitched roof of the River & Rowing Museum makes reference to the traditional wooden barns and boat-houses of Henley; the rest of the building is all invention. Its transparent open ground floor accommodates a café, shop, small galleries and meeting rooms; the first-floor boat halls floating above are closed boxes of oak lit only by ridged skylights, and house the main exhibition spaces. The building sits on a new raised ground plane that extends around it, like the platform around a Japanese temple. The design is a response both to a conservative planning environment that resisted any departure from comprehensible form, and to a local fear of new building *per se*. By combining the local vernacular with the ambitious manipulation of space and light, Chipperfield, in a rare UK project, has produced a building that local people seem to like, despite their fears.

This quite complex building leaves one with a memory of simplicity. The shell and its contents are articulated with an intense clarity. The form is intended to recall upturned boats and this really is the case, with the solid mass of oak-clad floor and the steeply sloping terned stainless steel roof, floating hull-like upside down over the glass-enclosed ground floor. From the outside, both from the tow-path and from the rear car park, one can see light and landscape beyond.

While the container is detailed with great clarity, the exhibition display (by other hands) is less so. In particular, in one of the two upper galleries the design of the suspension for the boats on display is somewhat heavy. Fortunately, the other gallery has been left more or less as built, a stunning high white space of pointed section, although even here long views are impeded by a (worthy) area designed for children. The circulation and the various ancillary areas are elegantly functional, and there is a particularly beautiful lift. The restaurant is a peaceful place, even though, oddly, it does not face the river. The flat-roofed annexe is approached via an elegant glazed bridge that maps the route of the Thames. Overall, the museum perfectly gathers the sense of the peaceful riverside. The building gives an impression of always having been there – not deferentially, but boldly.

ABOVE AND RIGHT David Chipperfield has kept the planners happy by making reference to the boat-houses of Henley, and has pleased an initially sceptical local population with a serene riverside destination.

OPPOSITE A partially glazed bridge links the two elements: the main boat-house structures and the box-like annexe.

CLIENT The River & Rowing Museum Foundation **STRUCTURAL ENGINEER** Whitbybird **CONTRACTOR** Norwest Holst Construction **CONTRACT VALUE** £6 million **PHOTOGRAPHER** Richard Bryant – Arcaid

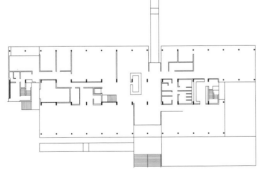

GROUND-FLOOR PLAN

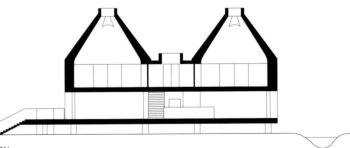

SECTION

STO MARKETING AND TRAINING BUILDING .STÜHLINGEN, GERMANY .MICHAEL WILFORD AND PARTNERS

WINNER OF THE RIBA COMMERCIAL AWARD

The Sto building announces itself to the world and to its village setting, close to the Swiss border, not only through the bold company logo on its roof but also through the dramatic parallelogram shape of its cantilevered four-storey office block. This block sits above a two-storey square base housing training facilities, to which it is connected by an oval entrance pavilion. The idea of building as statement is carried through in the use of the company's products throughout: the office block is surfaced with an insulated stucco system; curved blue metal panels are used in the opaque half of the reception oval; the lower walls are clad in square panels of grey basalt, with contrasting panels of coloured enamel. Inside, the reception area is a riot of colour, using Sto turquoise, orange and mauve finishes. Floors also show off company products.

The other reference made by the building is to naval architecture. The office block, with its blunt bows and stepped balconies at the stern, floats elegantly in the valley. The balconies provide sun decks for staff, with superb views of mountains and forest. The basement area, used for practical training in the use of products, is lit by continuous high windows and by the peeling-away of a section of the pavilion floor above. At ground-floor level, seminar rooms have flexible partitions and overlook a garden. An open well next to the stair allows light to flood through the building and provides views between levels.

This is a truly remarkable building both in and out of its context. The Sto company already dominates this small alpine village, and it has plans to grow still further. This is a company town, and the Sto logo shouts the fact from the roof-tops in vivid yellow lettering and in a way that could never happen in the United Kingdom. The lack of reticence in this setting could have been appalling had this been a less-good building. In fact, its very boldness shows that good design can transcend the need for a contextual approach. The striking geometry of the envelope is matched by the colourful brilliance of the interior. Here, as outside, the building acts as an advertising hoarding, with the clashing use of Sto finishes. The interior is tight, particularly in corridors and stairwells, but the apparently accidental juxtapositions of space and form are developed and organized to dramatic effect, especially in the foyer and at lower-ground-floor level, where the ovoid shafts would tempt any child or indeed any visitor to crawl. The exterior use of colour is perhaps less successful; already the mauve is beginning to fade in the southern sun, as it has at the Staatsgalerie in Stuttgart. But it is nothing that a fresh application of one of the company's products cannot put right.

ABOVE What would Jim have made of this? Stirling's former partner comes into his own with a landmark building that announces the company's wares to the world.

OPPOSITE Ahoy there! Good design transcends the need for contextualism in this nautical building.

AXONOMETRIC

CLIENT Sto **STRUCTURAL ENGINEER** Boll und Partner **CONTRACTOR** Züblin
CONTRACT VALUE DM15 million **PHOTOGRAPHER** Richard Bryant – Arcaid

STRATFORD REGIONAL STATION
.LONDON E15
.CHRIS WILKINSON ARCHITECTS
JOINT WINNER OF THE RIBA CIVIC AND COMMUNITY ARCHITECTURE AWARD

This is a beautifully simple solution to a very complex problem. Stratford station is a focal point for the regeneration of the Borough of Newham. As such, its ambitions are far greater than just to make the process of changing trains quicker and simpler. But it achieves both these aims supremely well. A mass of railway lines with completely different track orientations meet and cross here – one practical reason for the grand civic scale of this building. The station has an airport glamour about it, but, like an airport, it also has to be functional. A concrete subway under all the lines and a series of connecting stairs and escalators make interchange logical and straightforward. The space is formed by a cantilevered curved-shell steel envelope enclosed along its long edge and ends with structural-glass walls.

The geometry of the interior is effortless, allowing the rectangle of the main shell to control the varying angles produced by the relationship to the railway lines with a deft lightness of touch. The whole building is impeccably detailed. There is a sense that real experience in depth has been brought to bear on the handling and manufacture of all the elements. The result is a dramatic enclosure, all the more so in the context of Stratford. By day it is an evident grand new public space, and by night the lit underside of the shell transforms the structure into a gigantic light sculpture, inducing a sense of awe in all who see it.

Essentially, this is one huge curved shell of a canopy that swings up from the edge of the tracks and arches over the ticket hall, gates and the other paraphernalia of modern railways. The enclosure is completed by delicately detailed glazing that seems to gather up the exterior space of the plaza. The impact on the urban space is profound, according to passers-by who claim that the station has ennobled their bit of the town.

ABOVE The scale and grandeur of Wilkinson's transport interchange at Stratford will only make full sense with the coming of the 2012 Olympics. Someone must have tipped off the architects.

OPPOSITE The canopy swings up and over the ticket hall, providing shelter and drama.

SECTION

CLIENT London Underground STRUCTURAL ENGINEER Hyder Consulting
CONTRACTOR Kvaerner Construction CONTRACT VALUE £17 million
PHOTOGRAPHERS Dennis Gilbert – VIEW (opposite, bottom left and right)/
Timothy Soar (opposite, top)/Morley von Sternberg (above)

THE STIRLING PRIZE 1999
.AMANDA BAILLIEU

EDITOR OF THE *RIBA JOURNAL*

Each Stirling year begs comparison with the one before, or the one before that. Then, before you know it, there are 'vintage years' when the crop is so rich that it seems that every building on the shortlist could have been a winner. One of those vintage years was 1999, with buildings of exceptional quality. But it was also the last year that the judges didn't have to worry about the odd stray remark being pounced on to pep up television coverage. Neither did we need to have sound-bite reactions to buildings. We could take our time, and when we came to make the final difficult decision we didn't have to fit our deliberations around the TV schedules. Television has raised the profile not just of the prize itself but of architecture more generally, but in 1999 we could not have imagined how things were to change, and how fast.

Awards are only ever as good as the entries they attract. The reason this was such a memorable year, one of the best ever, was that it had such a range not only of type – from Tube stations to a parliament building – but also of architects. The shortlist reflected the incredible talent and diversity of British architecture, from its hero, Norman Foster, to Future Systems, the partnership of Jan Kaplicky and Amanda Levete, who hitherto had been unable to break into the big time. The NatWest Media Centre at Lord's was the big test, and if there had been a book open on which practice the profession wanted to win, Future Systems would have been the clear favourite.

And yet the new Jubilee line stations also had a strong case. Stations on new underground rail lines tend to be little more than expanded tunnels, but here were twelve different architectural solutions. Typically, perhaps, most of the discussion about the line had centred on its huge cost and the delays, and very little on the extraordinary architecture programme. We had two stations to look at (in future years other stations were to be on the shortlist). They were very different: the cavernous, almost bewitching North Greenwich station by Alsop Lyall & Störmer, and the clean-limbed, elegant Stratford regional station by Chris Wilkinson Architects.

Across the border there was the Museum of Scotland, the first major building by Gordon Benson and Alan Forsyth, commissioned in those far-off pre-National Lottery days through the competition system. Like Will Alsop's Peckham Library (winner of the Stirling Prize in 2000), the Museum of Scotland had an inauspicious start on the RIBA Awards circuit. Although it picked up an RIBA award, the regional jury felt the building was flawed and should not go forward for the Stirling Prize. This seemed incredible, and there was an overwhelming feeling among the national awards panel that it had to be given a second chance.

The other buildings on the shortlist were the Reichstag, Foster and Partners' sensitive restoration of Germany's most symbolic building as the country's new parliament; a school outside Dublin by the Irish practice O'Donnell + Tuomey; a headquarters building for the German company Sto by James Stirling's former partner Michael Wilford; and the River & Rowing Museum in Henley by David Chipperfield, one of Britain's most respected architects, who had had few opportunities to build in the United Kingdom.

Lord's was not everyone's first choice, but it was without doubt the building that had the most impact that year. However, it was more than just instant appeal that saw its main rival for the prize, the Museum of Scotland, come in a very close second. The judges were split three to two. Those supporting the museum had been enthralled by the architects' handling of materials, light and space, which produced a building of great power and complexity. Although it was

Benson + Forsyth's first major public building, it felt very mature, with every aspect – from the way exhibits are displayed to the curved cantilevered light-reflecting roof terrace – rigorously thought through.

It is often difficult to know what tips judges to favour one building when all are, in their way, so special. But we were captivated by the NatWest Media Centre, and we were equally captivated by the story behind it, which pitched the so-far unrecognized talents of Kaplicky and Levete against one of England's most venerable and strait-laced sporting institutions.

Although the criteria used for judging awards of this kind do not make allowance for any behind-the-scenes drama, the struggle to produce great architecture cannot be ignored: the arguments with clients and with contractors, the worries that this or that will be cut from the budget, the fevered battle with time constraints – all these things are what architecture is about. As the Scottish deputy arts minister, Rhona Brankin, said when she presented the prize at the Kelvingrove Art Gallery in Glasgow, "The making of good buildings – the creation of architecture – is a formidable task. It requires imagination, persistence, diplomacy and, often, sheer bloody-mindedness." Rarely have politicians been so honest about architecture.

Another reason why Lord's was the right choice was that it looked to the future in a way we could not have known at the time. It wasn't how it was built – this in fact was the least radical part of its programme – but what it said about architecture's power to convey an organization's message to the world. Of course, this wasn't new – architecture has always been used for brand enhancement – but Future Systems seemed to be going a step further: rather than denying the power of the media, the practice embraced it – a theme it was to explore further in its next major commission, the Selfridges store in Birmingham – in a way that was refreshingly bold and uncompromising.

Lord's is a great British institution, a private club for which you need to be entered almost at birth, with rules and dress codes, and where dukes and earls have watched their sons play cricket since the early nineteenth century. At the end of the twentieth century such institutions could no longer afford to stand still, but few were brave or canny enough to understand how architecture can change perceptions.

The building Lord's finally got was cheeky and irreverent, but also extraordinarily beautiful. And it is a building that does not communicate only with its members but also with millions of cricket fans around the world. There may not have been television cameras to record Kaplicky and Levete receiving their prize, but it did not matter. The building is on our screens every summer, reminding us, when we need it, that British architecture is no longer tweedy or sensible, but open, optimistic and, above all, fun.

2000

.JUDGES

Michael Manser Former RIBA president and chair of the RIBA Awards Group (chair)

Amanda Baillieu Editor of the *RIBA Journal*

Tracey Emin Artist

Amanda Levete Architect and Stirling Prize winner in 1999

Eric Parry Architect

.THE STIRLING PRIZE WINNER

.THE STIRLING PRIZE SHORTLIST

.THE STIRLING PRIZE 2000

PECKHAM LIBRARY AND MEDIA CENTRE .LONDON SE15 .ALSOP & STÖRMER

This was the third time Will Alsop had been shortlisted for the Stirling Prize, but it was his first victory. The library, part of the regeneration of Peckham, takes the form of a copper-clad L-shaped horizontal block (a giant rectangle with a bit cut out, according to Alsop) supported on a series of raking angled columns. The plan is practical since it avoids reducing access to the new public square, so people can use it day and night. In fact, the L defines a sheltered meeting area in front of the library so that it becomes a social hub rather than just a part of the streetscape. The stainless steel letters, each 2 metres high, announcing the building's function (the only things that could persuade you that this is a library), and an orange sunshield that looks like a beret or the flopping tongue of a hot dog, provide further drama. Two internal pods burst through the roof and add still more interest to the building's profile.

The library is Alsop & Störmer's imaginative response to the original brief, which was "to create a building of architectural merit that will bring prestige to the borough and a welcome psychological boost to the area. It should be a thoroughly modern building that is ahead of its time but also one that does not alienate people by giving an appearance of elitism, strangeness or exclusivity. Local people must be able to relate to the architecture and design as well as the services provided and they should feel pride in, affection for and ownership of the building." Peckham Library opened to the public in March 2000 and immediately attracted a very large number of users, including many new ones; more than one thousand were registered in the first three weeks.

This was a model brief and one that should be commended to all potential clients who want to commission award-winning buildings. However, if one had not read the brief, one could be excused for suspecting that response to function was not at the top of the architects' 'must-do' list. Nothing could be further from the truth: the library has a new, useful covered square at the entrance; it works internally in a very legible way; and the spaces are one delight after another, with drama never far away.

The following comments from the client best describe the library's success: "The building, with its extraordinary and innovative design, has impressed all who have seen it. In daily use it has fulfilled its brief as a practical working library and it is proving to be an exciting public space where people want to be. A spin-off benefit of the design and the very positive publicity it has attracted, is that it is helping to transform the image not only of Peckham, but of the public library service."

Peckham Library and Media Centre is a compelling piece of architecture. It was one of a number of buildings on the year's

CLIENT Southwark Education & Leisure Services **STRUCTURAL ENGINEER** Adams Kara Taylor **CONTRACTOR** Sunley Turin Construction **CONTRACT VALUE** £4.5 million **PHOTOGRAPHER** Roderick Coyne

shortlist that helped their building type to take a quantum leap forward (see also Sainsbury's and Canary Wharf). The library is in a tough neighbourhood, but the architects made a virtue of the fact, creating a security grille over the façade that is a thing of delicate beauty in itself, not least in the way it wraps around the underside of the canopy. To produce such an innovative and exciting piece of architecture against the uninspired and uninspiring backdrop of its immediate environs is a real achievement. To have done so on such a relatively low budget is even more remarkable.

At a tiny cost, this L-shaped box of copper and coloured glass has transformed part of an underprivileged borough. Tracey Emin, one of the Stirling judges, spent twelve years of her life in Peckham and was pleased to see money being spent there at last. She liked it because it didn't feel like a library, and she particularly liked the pods.

At 3.30 pm the building fills up with school kids. It makes an educational environment a cool place to go and be seen; this has to be some kind of architectural achievement. The building is full of bravado and as such has captured the hearts of a disaffected part of the population. All the best buildings are popular with their users, and the young people of Peckham flock into their library every day. In the end, this is a building to make you smile: more architecture should do that.

PAGES 106–107 Will Alsop's library for the people of Peckham comes into its own at night, proudly displaying the wares announced by the 2-metre-high lettering.

OPPOSITE AND BELOW The pods poke through the roof, adding interest to the profile already enlivened by the flopping orange tongue. Only Alsop could do this without being patronizing.

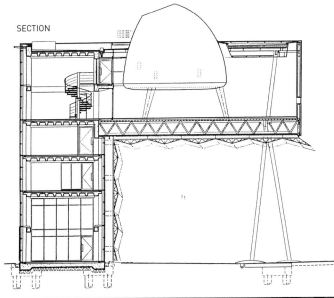

SECTION

THE BRITISH AIRWAYS LONDON EYE .LONDON SE1 .MARKS BARFIELD ARCHITECTS

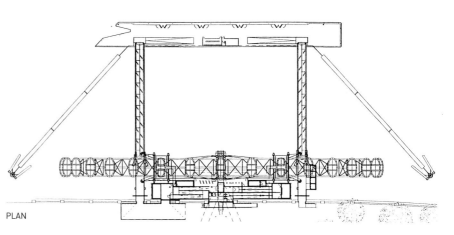

PLAN

The London Eye quickly became one of the symbols of the capital. The time between architects David Marks and Julia Barfield having the original idea and the giant wheel's final opening was a matter of years, but the construction was squeezed into just fourteen months, providing a further challenge to an already monumental engineering job.

The wheel is supported on one side only on a tilted A-frame. Its rim is cantilevered out over the Thames, with the hub rotating on a cast-iron spindle. Everything about the thirty-two capsules, each of which carries twenty-five passengers, is designed to enhance the experience: the clarity of the glass, the solidity of the central benches and the smoothness of the ride, achieved by internal drive motors that keep the capsules steady and horizontal, even in high winds, as the wheel rotates.

The list of superlatives is endless: the Eye is the largest object ever lifted from the horizontal to the vertical, and the third-tallest structure in Britain; the hub is the largest single steel casting ever, and so on. But most significantly, as the judges predicted, the Eye is clearly the one addition to London's skyline that has had as much impact as Eiffel's tower had on Paris's. The chances are that, despite its limited planning life, it will be around for as long.

What is most important about the Eye is that two truly creative architects came up with the idea and the design, found the place, and selected the client. This sent out the message that architects have to get out there and sell their ideas, carry them through and then get a share of the equity in return. The Eye inspires, it is ambitious, it is beautiful and it works, which is what we expect from an award winner. What is more, it gives Londoners and visitors a viewing platform the city previously lacked. Now every capital city will want one.

The Stirling judges wondered: is it a building? Is it a bird? Is it a plane? The Eye is all those in terms of the views it provides of the capital. For first-time riders, even for vertigo sufferers, it is a thrill to be edged smoothly skywards, so that the archaeology of the Festival of Britain, then the whole city, spreads out below. From here it's possible to see everything that is right about London and a lot of what is wrong. Planners, as well as architects, should be forced to take this ride. The Eye is a superlative piece of architecture-cum-engineering that has won the hearts of Londoners and visitors in a way that no other millennial building has. As much as overturning preconceived notions about contextualism – how can views be interrupted if you can see through the structure? – it represents a shift in the public's view of architecture. In a way it is a return to the brash self-confidence of the Victorians; it certainly would not have been built ten years earlier on so significant a site.

ABOVE The Eye is a piece of architecture-cum-engineering that has challenged all notions of contextualism.

OPPOSITE This giant wheel has changed the way people see London – in plan instead of as a series of elevations.

CLIENT British Airways London Eye Company **STRUCTURAL ENGINEERS** Babtie Allott & Lomax/Hollandia/Infragroep/Ove Arup & Partners **CONTRACTOR** Mace **CONTRACT VALUE** Undisclosed **PHOTOGRAPHER** Nick Wood

CANARY WHARF UNDERGROUND STATION .LONDON E14 .FOSTER AND PARTNERS

At 300 metres long, Canary Wharf is the largest of the stations on the Jubilee line extension. It is built in a pre-existing drained dock. Above ground, simple, elegant glazed canopies are cut into grassy banks set in a small park. By day these admit daylight; at night they glow with inner light. Twenty escalators descend into the cavern, with steel and glass ticket offices and administrative offices at one level and trains at the next. The exposed concrete of the walls and the soaring pillars are of a quality that is as beautiful as it is robust.

The dramatic journey down the escalators takes the traveller into a contemporary cathedral of a space bathed in natural light. Even on the final descent to platform level there is a sense that some natural light is permeating down. Underground stations are dirty places, with the rush of displaced air carrying the general detritus of London life. To make a place that can be so easily cleaned and maintained is no small achievement; this will look good for years.

It would be easy to become blasé about the work of Foster and Partners. The practice is so prolific and the projects so important that one is tempted to demand more from Foster than from others. Canary Wharf station is a masterpiece; it addresses and solves all its problems effortlessly. This is a precisely organized, elegant and simple station, more like a main railway terminus than a Tube station. What impresses is the way it has been thought out and carried through. To move such vast numbers of people – 60,000 a day at opening, rising to 100,000 – is no mean achievement; Foster and Partners has made it all look so simple.

This is the product of a practice at the peak of its powers. The architects may have had a blank canvas to work on – unlike, say, those at Westminster or Stratford stations – but they have created a masterpiece on it. From the elegant canopies – mini-Duxfords, they were dubbed 'Fosteritos' when trialled on the Bilbao Metro – down to the detailing at platform level, everything is exquisitely done. But it is the great hall with its soaring slender columns that most inspires awe and admiration. At present only one entrance is in use, but when its mirror opposite is open and people stream down the matching sets of escalators to merge in the vast ticket hall, the full drama of the place will be revealed. Tube stations are not usually exciting; they are meant to be functional. This one manages to be both.

If the King's Cross fire had happened here, no one would have died. That is architecture that works.

ABOVE The scheme makes full use of the opportunity for drama provided by the drained dock.

OPPOSITE This is the nearest Norman Foster has yet come to building a cathedral; Canary Wharf has the grace and majesty of a Coventry, even a Durham.

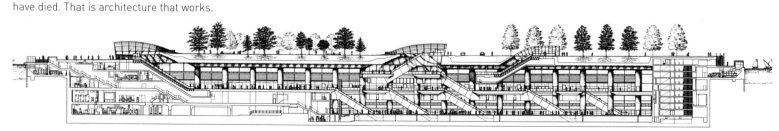

LONG SECTION

CLIENT London Underground **STRUCTURAL ENGINEER** Ove Arup & Partners
CONTRACTOR Tarmac Bachy Joint Venture **CONTRACT VALUE** £32.5 million
PHOTOGRAPHER Dennis Gilbert – VIEW

GSW HEADQUARTERS
.BERLIN, GERMANY .SAUERBRUCH HUTTON ARCHITECTS

This is not just a green building, it is most of the other colours in the rainbow too. When the sun comes out and the blinds close between the double skin of the curved façade of the new tower, it looks like a pick-and-mix paint chart, but prettier.

The eye-catching scheme is centred on an early 1960s tower block that was opened by Willy Brandt when he was mayor of Berlin. The block formed the headquarters of GSW, the city's housing association. The winning entry in a competition launched shortly after reunification retained the original seventeen-storey block and added a curved twenty-two-storey block, no more than 11.5 metres wide, that enables generous daylighting and natural ventilation. In addition, there is a three-storey pillbox, and a curved building, 114 metres long, that follows the line of the street and provides shopping as well as offices. The project's low-energy concept is claimed to reduce consumption by 40 per cent, with a double-glass façade containing coloured blinds and a windsail on top of the 81-metre-high building being key features.

Ecological considerations are an integral part of the design. The outer skin acts as a warm pullover in winter, while absorbing heat in the summer. People can control their own environment by opening windows or operating blinds. Natural ventilation is supplemented by a mechanical system in winter.

The building seeks to work with the physical structure and memories of the site. It succeeds unequivocally. The qualities of the new building not only successfully integrate the original building into a functional whole but also respond to the layers of this area of Berlin by reinforcing city scale and edges, by relating to adjacent buildings and by creating urban landmarks. The building represents a skilful and thoughtful 'stitching' exercise.

What is perhaps most impressive is the way the architects have taken the neglected high-rise block and created a whole new composition – a collage of buildings – around it. This is what so much architecture is today: dealing with existing buildings in the middle of cities and coming up with responses that add to the original and add to the life of the city. This scheme sets a benchmark for inner-city regeneration. Office buildings don't often excite, but this is a really exciting building. It could have been a huge bombastic structure that was entirely inappropriate for a client with a social remit. Instead, the architects have come up with a building that is totally usable and very beautiful.

The Stirling judges marvelled at the generosity of the corridors, at the opening windows on the twenty-second floor and, last but not least, at the atrium, the gentle curve of which picks up the line of the street. It is lined with etched-glass doors leading to lettable office spaces, and ends in a mirror that doubles visual value for money.

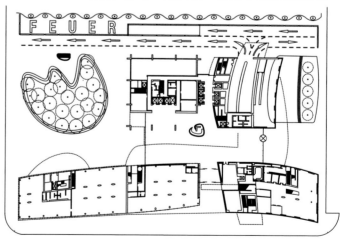

GROUND-FLOOR PLAN

CLIENT Gemeinnützige Siedlungs- und Wohnungsbaugesellschaft (GSW)
STRUCTURAL AND ENVIRONMENTAL ENGINEERS Arup GmbH/ARGE Arup GmbH with
IgH mbH CONTRACTORS Züblin/Bilfinger Berger CONTRACT VALUE £58 million
PHOTOGRAPHERS Bitter Bredt (above; opposite)/Annette Kisling (top)

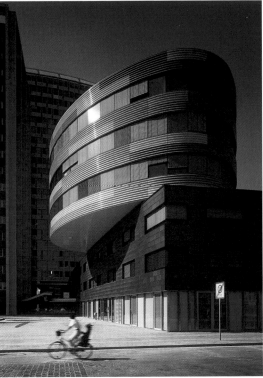

OPPOSITE Sauerbruch Hutton, with its first Stirling-shortlisted project, solved a common problem: how to deal with existing city-centre buildings, using architecture to add to the life of the city.

ABOVE AND RIGHT There is a refreshing and exciting naivety about the almost child-like use of building blocks and colour.

NEW ART GALLERY WALSALL
.WALSALL, WEST MIDLANDS
.CARUSO ST JOHN ARCHITECTS

The gallery was the result of a competitive process, from which the then young and relatively inexperienced team of Adam Caruso and Peter St John emerged and began a close and highly productive collaboration with the enthusiastic gallery director, Peter Jenkinson. The form of the building – a six-storey, terracotta-clad tower, 30 metres high – gives the town a landmark building and allows the various parts of the gallery to be accommodated separately. Each space is side-lit but on a different scale: the Garman Ryan suite has small windows suited to the domestic nature of the collection; the main exhibition galleries have flexible clerestorey lighting that can be blacked out to accommodate video installations. A choice of lifts or stairs from the dramatic black-concrete-floored entrance hall not only improves access, but means no prescribed route is laid down. The fine shuttered concrete, best seen in the entrance hall and the top-floor café, was produced using the same timber as was used for the interior cladding, giving a pleasing unity to the whole.

The public space outside is almost as important to the town as the gallery itself. Lead consultant for this part of the project was artist Richard Wentworth. He has edged a newly created canal basin with a black-and-white chequerboard path and carried this through into the funnel-shaped square, across which the gallery outfaces the uninspired Post-modernity of new Woolworths and BHS stores. The gallery itself picks up on its high-street context with a shop window that is used to sample the exhibitions inside.

Inside, the gallery is full of surprises, from the Noddy Holder lift announcements (the Slade star is a native of the town) to the way in which the coolness of the foyer gives way to the warm intimacy of the domestically scaled wood-clad rooms that provide the perfect home for the Epsteins. The windows, apparently random from the outside, work from the inside out, framing views of the town like works of art. It is a serene and comfortable space to be in. The domestic scale of its spaces helps to connect the gallery with the community. It is not patronizing, it is not in any way dumbed-down. The importance of this building is as much social as it is aesthetic. That an arts building – particularly one outside London – should not compromise on quality of materials or execution sends out the clear message that we no longer need to accept second best when it comes to funding and accommodating the arts. That will be the Lottery's most lasting legacy. Ultimately, this building says that every marginalized part of Britain should and can have first-class architecture.

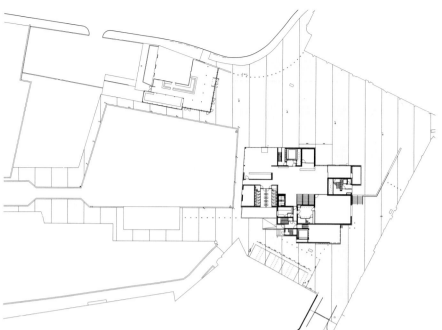

SITE PLAN

ABOVE The New Art Gallery Walsall was one of the stars of Lottery funding. It has made a real place out of a forlorn part of town.

OPPOSITE The gallery sends a clear message that arts buildings, wherever they are, can and should be properly funded.

CLIENT Walsall Metropolitan Borough Council **STRUCTURAL ENGINEER** Ove Arup & Partners **CONTRACTOR** Sir Robert McAlpine **CONTRACT VALUE** £21 million **PHOTOGRAPHER** Hélène Binet

SAINSBURY'S SUPERMARKET
.LONDON SE10
.CHETWOOD ASSOCIATES

The architects worked for four years with Sainsbury's to develop a model low-energy supermarket before winning the tender from English Partnerships to build it on the Greenwich Peninsula. In use, the supermarket rates as 'excellent', according to the exacting standards of environmental assessment developed by the Building Research Establishment, using 50 per cent less energy than a standard store.

A steel-framed, 280-metre-radius vaulted roof, with integrated north-light double-glazed strips, is supported on perimeter reinforced concrete walls that provide thermal mass and resist the pressure of earth-sheltered grassy banks. Fresh air is drawn into the building through the void under a suspended floor via large pipes buried in the embankments. Automatically operated external aluminium louvres control daylight and solar gain; recessed lighting in the ceiling responds to the amount of natural light entering the building.

This exemplary exercise combines sensible use of technology with an imaginative redefinition of the nature of a supermarket space. One is immediately struck by the calm comfort of the place; even on a hot day the interior environment is ideal. Artificial lighting is by concealed fittings on the merchandizing gondolas, which means that the most important objects receive the most light; the store does not have the 'white-out' feeling of most supermarkets, overlit by rows and rows of suspended fluorescents; and less energy is used. There are too many energy-saving sustainable ideas to list here; this is a pioneering project that must be repeated elsewhere. As the People's Choice this was the surprise member of the shortlist, but it proved to be a very worthy one. One of the RIBA's criteria is that a building should be excellent of its type. This one went far beyond that: it is an excellent building. And as a supermarket, it is outstanding.

In spirit, this building is more like a covered market than a supermarket in that it looks back as well as forward. Overall, this is a huge step for a supermarket, a building type that does not generally excite. It is interesting not just for its architecture but also for the way it redefines what supermarkets could be in the future. Shoppers, staff, judges and the Channel 4 voters all concurred that this was a building well deserving of its place on the Stirling Prize shortlist.

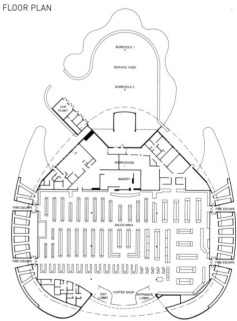

FLOOR PLAN

CLIENT Sainsbury's Supermarkets STRUCTURAL ENGINEER WSP Consulting Engineers ENVIRONMENTAL ENGINEERS Max Fordham & Partners/Oscar Faber CONTRACTOR RGCM CONTRACT VALUE £13 million PHOTOGRAPHER Richard Glover – VIEW

ABOVE This Sainsbury's uses half the energy of most supermarkets, and that is not because of the windmills but because of good design and an environmental strategy that was fully supported by an enthusiastic client.

OPPOSITE From the air, the supermarket all but disappears into the landscape; internally, there is a use of daylight rare in this type of building.

88 WOOD STREET
.LONDON EC2
.RICHARD ROGERS PARTNERSHIP

RRP's first City building since Lloyd's is a lettable block for an international finance house, Daiwa Europe. It is very different from the headquarters building commissioned before the Far East recession. But within the constraints of the speculative office brief, this makes a very special contribution to the City of London. It rises in three linked steps of ten, fourteen and eighteen storeys, complementing London Wall at one end and a Wren church tower in Wood Street at the other. Trademark external bracing, Dome-yellow steelwork for the structure and blue and red for services add to the drama of the building. Triple glazing is used everywhere apart from the north aspect, which is double glazed. The glass is highly specified: an ultra-transparent low-iron glass with all the green removed, adding £750,000 to the overall cost. This was the first time it had been used in a major building. All windows are fitted with automatic blinds that respond to sunlight to reduce solar gain.

Instead of a Lloyd's-type atrium, Wood Street has a double-height lobby that passers-by can enjoy. It features a 54-metre wall running the length of the building. Panoramic circulation towers link the office floors, and there are roof terraces on three levels with spectacular views of the City. The lifts are among the fastest and smoothest in the country.

The judges' unanimous view was that this commercial office building is a practical, simple and elegant structure, neatly slipped into a confined site, deferring to the surrounding buildings, including the tower that is all that remains of Wren's St Alban Church. A high quality of detail is consistently maintained, and the mechanical services incorporate extensive energy-conservation measures. An excellent workplace has been created with maximum daylight and generous views out towards the City, behind twentieth-century façades in traditional principles of geometry.

The original competition entry would itself have made a fine addition to the cityscape, but troubles with the Far Eastern economy meant that client Daiwa no longer required this as a headquarters building. RRP's second solution was still more inspired than its first. What it has produced, under Graham Stirk's direction, is one of the firm's finest buildings, demonstrating that sometimes a difficult process leads to the best product.

This is the culmination of thirty years of work for the Richard Rogers Partnership: the regular module, ways of getting light into a building, the exploitation of glass; everything is explored and carried through, coming together in a beautifully detailed and serene whole. One only needs to look around at other speculative offices in the City to see just how far this pushes forward the type.

GROUND-FLOOR PLAN

CLIENT Daiwa Europe STRUCTURAL ENGINEER Ove Arup & Partners
CONTRACTOR Kajima UK Engineering CONTRACT VALUE £55 million
PHOTOGRAPHERS Richard Bryant – Arcaid (above)/Katsuhisa Kida (opposite)

OPPOSITE TOP RRP's first building in the City of London since Lloyd's makes a special contribution to the fragmented skyline.

OPPOSITE BOTTOM AND RIGHT Wood Street bears many of the hallmarks of RRP's work but shows how the practice has entered the mainstream by producing what turned out to be a speculative office block.

THE STIRLING PRIZE 2000
.JAY MERRICK
ARCHITECTURE CORRESPONDENT OF *THE INDEPENDENT*

In the last year of the twentieth century British architecture produced a Stirling Prize shortlist of such extraordinary ripeness and invention that one stifles the urge to reach for a copy of one of Robert Parker's magisterial guides to the wines of Bordeaux to filch a handful of his adjectives. For this was the year that the award of the Stirling Prize seemed singular in two senses.

Ask any critic, or bring the subject up with any architect in his or her mid-thirties, and the polemics – if not sudden expletive furies – surface. Why? Because most of the seven finalists had a strong and distinct claim to British architecture's premier gong in what had been, rather aptly, the Chinese year of the dragon. There were six different building types in the mix, which meant that this *fin-de-siècle* prize would send a very particular – and perhaps reductive – signal about the future of our architecture to a public that had become increasingly interested in this area of creative endeavour. But which signal? And why, on this richly endowed occasion, just one? If the great Oscar Niemeyer had to share the 1988 Pritzker Prize with the corporately creative Gordon Bunshaft, couldn't one or two more Stirling Prizes have been minted in 2000?

Here, after all, was a shortlist with something fascinatingly divisive about it: seven practices and seven projects that gave form to ambitious architectural futures rather than glibly recycled versions of the past. It was very difficult to see a clear winner, or even to compare virtues. When one considered the architecture, it was obvious that judgemental relativity was only possible in one instance, involving two buildings: Richard Rogers Partnership's 88 Wood Street and Sauerbruch Hutton's GSW headquarters in Berlin.

My personal distillate contained four of the official seven buildings and one more, from outside the main prize shortlist. There was, I thought, a putatively decisive winning case to be made for these five buildings.

Each of the practices involved had offered up its best work for some time. There was no question of subtle extra weightings based on 'big names' and the aura of their past work; the quality of the individual buildings made that kind of baggage redundant. This wasn't the architectural equivalent of Sugar Ray Leonard versus a string of Dave 'Boy' Greens from the Lincolnshire Fens. It was big-hitting clones of Leonard, Tommy 'The Motor City Cobra' Hearns and 'Marvellous' Marvin Hagler in the ring at the same time. Quite predictably, the jury's deliberations were themselves something of a rumble.

Six of the seven buildings on the shortlist offered sharply composed essays in Modernism; the seventh, Chetwood Associates' Sainsbury's supermarket at Greenwich, addressed the appetite for food and fossil-fuel consumption, and the building's appearance set the stage for subsequent 'environmental' architecture on Stirling Prize shortlists that have moved this particularly fraught technical game on considerably. That the Modernism on show seemed to have a shock-of-the-new vibe about it said a great deal about the architects involved because their glimpses into the future were not so much strokes of blue-sky genius as acts of extreme refinement and, in some cases, remarkable beauty.

Richard Rogers Partnership's 88 Wood Street radiated a clarity of form, relative scale and detail that seemed to be a perfecting of Walter Gropius's Bauhaus industrialism. This set an architectural standard in British medium-rise office accommodation that has yet to be surpassed. One looks forward to the apotheosis of this particular architectural method when the practice's 122 Leadenhall Street tower is completed.

Foster and Partners' Canary Wharf Underground station delivered another kind of perfection. The V-bomber blister-canopy architecture that the practice had delivered with such assurance at the American Air Museum in Duxford was now fused to London's greatest modern experiment in financial place-making. We've seen its svelte canopies before – but not those beautiful vaults, into which one ascends, in a peculiarly evolutionary way, from the humming darkness deep in the London clay to daily obeisance in a place where, as the American novelist Jay McInerney put it so well, brightness falls.

We'd seen nothing like the BA London Eye, either – a cyclic brightness, the rise of which is perpetually and precisely matched by its fall. Marks Barfield Architects posed an interesting problem with this structure. It was so brilliantly *other*, and such an immediate popular success, that it was already a winning piece of international architecture. The quality of its design, the superb engineering, the delightful *coup de foudre* of its very raising, meant that it had to be shortlisted. But how to compare almost pure structure against architectural 'containers'?

These three projects proved that Modernism could be unquestionably beautiful. And that's why, despite the architectural precedents that informed them, they seemed just as new and refreshing as the genuinely extraordinary Kielder Belvedere, Northumberland, by Softroom Architects, a titchy architectural ingot that's a protean metaphorical riddle and was winner of the year's Stephen Lawrence Prize. Modernist certainly – but from where, exactly? Mars? An Italian outsize pasta factory with chrome-plating facilities? A stealth tank manufacturer?

Will Alsop's winning Peckham Library is not exactly beautiful, and not exactly from Mars. Yet, like most of the shortlisted projects, it seemed new and surprising. There was about it an aura of the architect's Cardiff Bay Visitor Centre – not literally, but in the same cursory and decisive act of form-making, the effect of which was very powerfully magnified by its *tabula rasa* site in south London.

The reinvention of the architectural antecedents of the New Art Gallery Walsall, by Caruso St John Architects, was perhaps even more remarkable. The gallery's boldness and power lay in its restraint and in the extraordinary atmosphere generated by its volumes and programme. In a manner that suggested a fusion of Kahn and Wright, the building was something rare in a hyperbolic age of icons and eye-cons: a piece of don't-look-at-me architecture that turns out to be grippingly, and humanely, engaging.

What a year, what a box of delights! And what a pity that, in 2000, public consumption of the Stirling Prize tended to be focused on just one building.

2001

.JUDGES

Marco Goldschmied Former RIBA president (chair)

Will Alsop Architect and Stirling Prize winner in 2000

Paul Finch Publisher of *The Architects' Journal*

Alice Rawsthorn Director of the Design Museum

Janet Street-Porter Journalist and broadcaster

.THE STIRLING PRIZE WINNER

.THE STIRLING PRIZE SHORTLIST

.THE STIRLING PRIZE 2001

Marco Goldschmied Former RIBA president (chair)

MAGNA SCIENCE ADVENTURE CENTRE
.ROTHERHAM, SOUTH YORKSHIRE
.WILKINSON EYRE ARCHITECTS

The conversion of this former steelworks was a major Millennium project, additionally funded by English Partnerships and the European Regional Development Fund. Two bays, each 350 metres long, make up the cathedral-like shed. When constructed, during World War I, it was the biggest building in Europe, but it is the interior that is truly awe-inspiring. The design retains and enhances the excitement of the space and puts it to use to house exhibitions relating to the four elements of the steel-making process: earth, air, fire and water. The areas are linked by walkways and bridges. Artefacts from the building's past are retained as evocative sculptures, while video walls recall the human story of steel-making, most compellingly in the vast, quadruple-height entrance hall, where the original building is left to do all the work, aided only by a few audio-visual tricks. Elsewhere the interventions are more conventionally architectural and house the four exhibition pavilions.

Rarely do architects get to work on a project of such vast scale as an abandoned steelworks. Here, the architects have responded with suitably gigantic gestures, but also with an attention to detail in the exhibition areas, combining a necessary robustness with invention and surprise. The integration of architecture, interactive exhibits and highly effective lighting and sound design is relatively seamless, so that visitors oscillate between the compact educational experiences of the fire, earth, water and air pavilions and revealed fragments of the vastness of the old steelworks. This is exhilarating and releases a sense of awe and excitement in all who visit. Photographs cannot convey the feeling of being inside. The drama of being a small person within a vast black space that is relieved only by gashes of red light, sheets of flame and spots of white light has to be experienced.

Wilkinson Eyre's great achievement, supported by inspired exhibition and lighting design, has been to allow the existing building to speak for itself and to tell its own history. The simple device of inserting a walkway that runs centrally through space along the length of the building keeps visitors away from the dirty tackiness of an industrial building only recently abandoned and allows them to savour its vastness and equally to find their way easily to the exhibits, with the sense of being on a conducted tour. These more orchestrated experiences are handled with panache, but architecturally they are subservient to the experience of the whole. The result has the obvious rightness that can only be achieved by an inspired and experienced team working with a single-minded client who supported them.

The scheme has subsequently been criticized for its disappointing visitor numbers. There are a number of issues

CLIENT The Magna Trust STRUCTURAL ENGINEER Mott MacDonald EXHIBITION DESIGN Event Communications LIGHTING DESIGN Speirs & Major CONTRACTOR Schal CONTRACT VALUE £37.2 million PHOTOGRAPHER Benedict Luxmoore

PAGES 126–27 From the outside this former steelworks – the biggest building in Europe when it was built during World War I – is little changed. That is an important architectural decision in itself.

ABOVE AND OPPOSITE The drama is saved for the inside, with four new pods housing exhibitions based on the four elements used in steel manufacture. But even here the art, practised by all the designers involved, is to draw attention to the building itself.

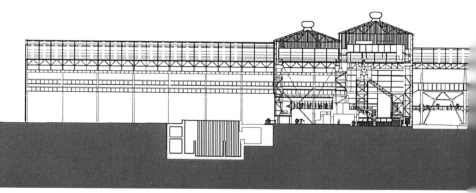

SECTION

here. First, it is in the nature of the Lottery: applicants for funds are all but obliged to exaggerate the number of anticipated visits in order to get funding. Secondly, as any director of any visitor attraction, be it a museum or a funfair, will confirm, attendances invariably drop after the initial six- to twelve-month honeymoon period (most people visit a venue just once). Thirdly, there is the matter of scale: Magna is nearly half a kilometre long; drop a thousand visitors into it (the daily average) and they all but disappear. Only inside the four pavilions are the numbers apparent; in fact, at times these spaces can seem cramped. Staff have complained of the lack of office accommodation inside the main shed (they are housed in another building some way away), but there are good conservation reasons for this: a series of windows punched in the steel skin to admit daylight would have ruined the industrial aesthetic. As it is, the exterior is remarkably little changed from the time when this was the most productive steelworks in the country. A final criticism has concerned indoor winter temperatures, which are so cold you can see your breath. But then, Magna was designed and is marketed as an outdoor attraction. Perhaps the architects got the idea from another Stirling Prize winner, Norman Foster's American Air Museum at Duxford (1998), which does the same thing with considerably less justification given the vast difference in the buildings' respective volumes.

There is about Magna a modesty that, done by other hands, might have been self-indulgent. Chris Wilkinson and Jim Eyre are generous enough to hand credit to others, in particular to Event for its spectacular shows, to which their architecture is a backdrop; to Jonathan Speirs for lighting structure and exhibits with such invention and panache; to their structural engineer, this time Mott MacDonald, for realizing and releasing the potential of this complex structure; but most of all to the unsung and unknown designers and builders of this vast shed and its original contents, which are, even now, the stars of the show.

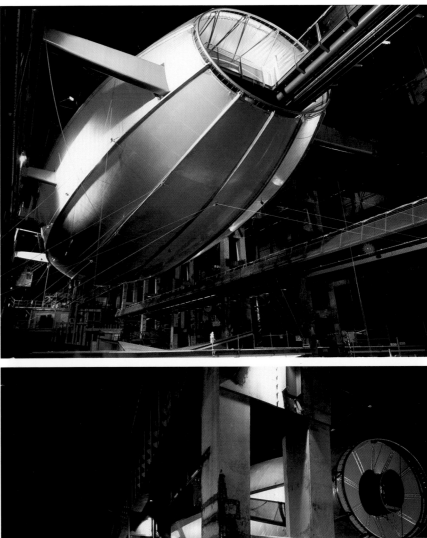

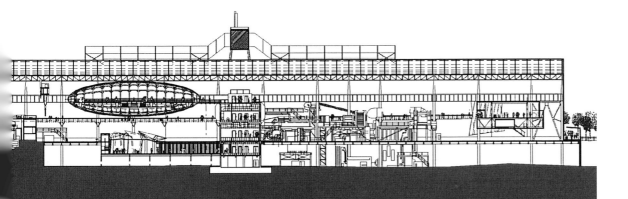

BRITISH EMBASSY .BERLIN, GERMANY .MICHAEL WILFORD AND PARTNERS

Michael Wilford's new British Embassy in Berlin is a flagship twice over. The architect was asked to design a building to fly the flag for a modern, approachable Britain; he was also subsequently required to design a flagship for the Private Finance Initiative. Both the project and its means of delivery were inherited from the previous Conservative administration and carried out enthusiastically by the Labour government. It is to Wilford's credit that he has carried it off so consummately well and shown that PFI can be made to work. But there is a caveat: the architect was appointed long before the means of procurement was decided, and it was only his determination to see his competition-winning designs through to completion without major compromise that made the project work so well.

Throughout the Cold War, Wilhelmstrasse stood on the edge of a no-man's-land. Now it is regaining some of its former glory as a street of palaces, courtyards and gardens. The British Embassy forms a distinctive part of this regeneration. It takes the idea of the Berlin courtyard, with gates leading on to an elegant court just big enough to turn a Rolls-Royce in. Inside, a grand staircase leads up to a *piano nobile*. This winter garden forms the heart of the building, with sunshine flooding through roof lights, lighting the artworks and Wilford's hallmark colours. Conference rooms, dining-rooms and offices are arranged simply around this space.

The city's planning guidelines determined the full-width sandstone façade, but Wilford has subverted this with a collage of coloured forms projecting into the street, making passers-by intrigued about what is going on inside and saying, perhaps, something about Britain today.

The building is the product of a mature architectural talent applied to a very testing site and brief. Caught between the constraints of history, contemporary city-development guidelines and an evolving political drama, it has managed to fulfil an appropriate level of decorum while also being characterful.

The site is penned in by party walls on all but the Wilhelmstrasse frontage. The volumetric and spatial resolution is excellent, maximizing the public domain to reflect a culture of 'openness' and reinterpreting the traditional elements of the court, stair, hall and reception room in an inventive sequence that avoids the potential dumbness of pure architectural formality by a successful dialogue with outstanding artworks by, among others, David Tremlett, Tony Cragg, Anish Kapoor and Peter Sedgley.

The Wilhelmstrasse façade expresses the sectional articulation of the building and is a bold and engaging composition, where it might easily have become dour and over-monumental.

ABOVE Internally, Wilford's embassy is not only a showcas[e] British artistic talent; it is a compelling work of art in itse[lf].

LEFT AND OPPOSITE Externally, the architects have subverte[d] the heavy façade insisted on by the planners with cuts an[d] projections that say as much about Britain as do the artworks inside.

CLIENT Overseas Estate Department, Foreign & Commonwealth Office **STRUCTURAL AND MECHANICAL ENGINEERS** Whitbybird with Boll und Partner/Jaeger, Mornhinweg + Partner **CONTRACTOR** Bilfinger Berger **CONTRACT VALUE** PFI project – final figure unknown **PHOTOGRAPHER** Peter Cook – VIEW

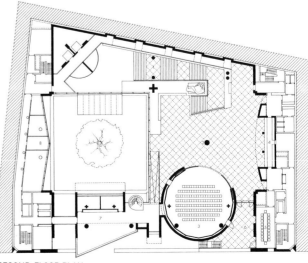

SECOND-FLOOR PLAN

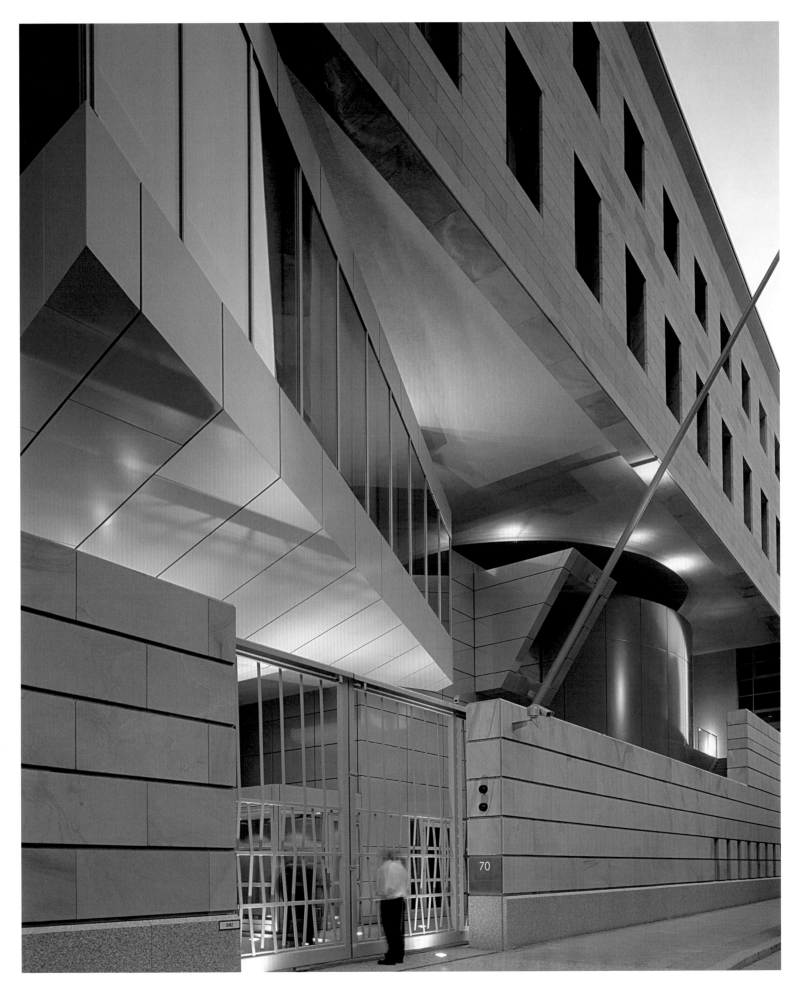

EDEN PROJECT
.ST AUSTELL, CORNWALL .NICHOLAS GRIMSHAW & PARTNERS

A £57 million Millennium project, the Eden Project is a showcase for global biodiversity. It comprises three main elements: the interlinked biomes, geodesic domes inspired by Buckminster Fuller (with more to follow); a link building; and a hilltop visitor centre. Together the biomes form the largest plant enclosure in the world. To ensure the maximum amount of daylight for the plants, the positioning of the biomes was determined by solar modelling and they are clad in lightweight ETFE.

The visitor centre curves to follow the contours of the site and provides ticketing, a café, a shop and an education facility. It is echoed in the green-roofed link building at the base of the quarry, which provides bridge access into the two biomes, as well as restaurant facilities (already inadequate given vastly higher than anticipated visitor numbers even at the time of judging). The biomes are entered directly from this space.

The Eden Project is the successful realization of a dream that has long haunted modern architects: the artificial world enclosed under a single, vast roof. Based on an original concept by architect Jonathan Ball working with co-client Tim Smit, and designed by Nicholas Grimshaw, it has been realized through the ingenuity of that doyen of structural engineering, Tony Hunt. Set

at the bottom of a redundant clay quarry, the Eden Project's giant biomes allow two artificial environments – one rainforest, one Mediterranean climate – to flourish on a scale that dwarfs any traditional palm house.

Grimshaw's domes do look back to the ideas of the visionary architect Buckminster Fuller, inventor of the geodesic dome. But while Fuller's domes were inherently inflexible circles or sections of circles, Grimshaw has combined the geodesic dome in varied sections to create a roof that can be adapted to cover any shape. From outside, the building appears an intriguingly alien eruption out of the valley bottom. Within, it has a sense of scale that few modern buildings achieve. It is a remarkable technical feat.

The approach to the building is full of surprise: it is simply not visible in long views above the lip of the quarry. The technical complexity is self-evident but the solutions so well judged as to appear effortless. There is an awesome sense of place in a site defined as much by the external space as by the buildings themselves. Fuller's vision of huge areas covered in a diaphanous structure was never so fully realized.

It is a truth all but universally accepted that this is the finest project in the first decade of the award not to have won the Stirling Prize.

ABOVE Few architects get the chance to play God; fewer still could seize the chance and build a little world.

OPPOSITE Nicholas Grimshaw's genius has taken Buckminster Fuller's rigid geodesic dome and varied the sections to create a roof flexible enough to cover any shape.

CLIENT Eden Project STRUCTURAL ENGINEER Anthony Hunt Associates
CONTRACTORS Sir Robert McAlpine/Alfred McAlpine Construction
CONTRACT VALUE £57 million PHOTOGRAPHER Peter Cook – VIEW

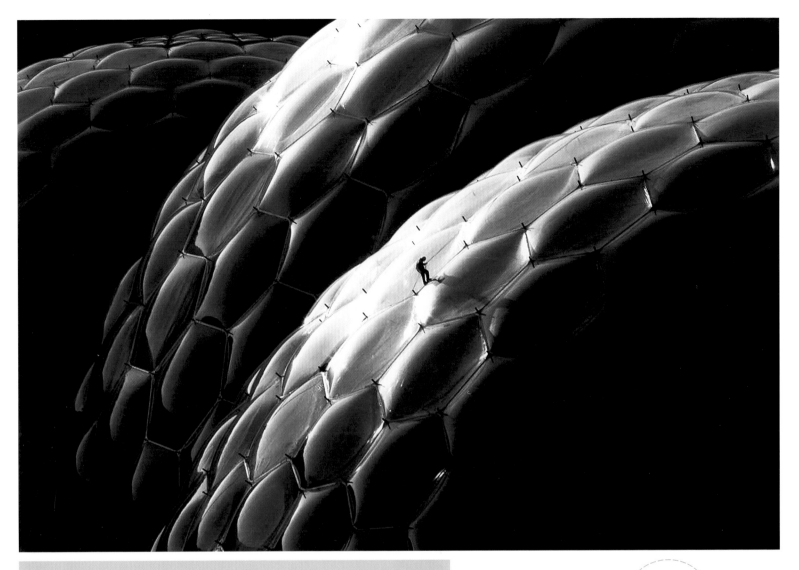

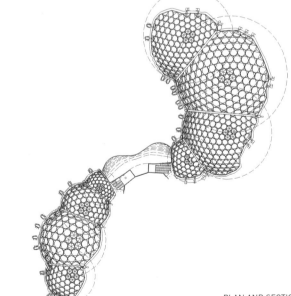

PLAN AND SECTION

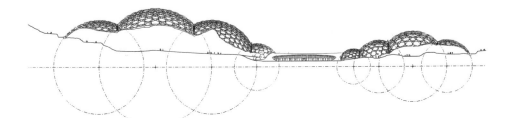

THE LAWNS
.LONDON N6 .ELDRIDGE SMERIN

Needing increased living space and improved access to their garden, Frances and John Sorrell set Nick Eldridge and Piers Smerin their first challenge as a practice. The resulting design wraps round the 1950s house by Leonard Manasseh, doubling its size with double-height mainly glazed extensions and a dramatic glazed studio box replacing the pitched roof.

Eldridge Smerin's initial response to the brief had a double impact: it convinced the clients to buy a house they were unsure about, and it persuaded the architects to make the leap from the security of an established UK architectural practice (John McAslan + Partners) to become principals of their own studio.

In response to the clients' requirements for an increase in living space and an improvement in the relationship of the house to the garden, the architects have not only added the glazed extensions; at the same time, the integration of the house and the site has been fundamentally readdressed. The relationship of the living-rooms to the south-facing garden has been successfully managed. Here the original elevation is left intact in order to contrast with the glass extensions on either side. To the entrance court from the street, on the other hand, the house presents a dramatic new 'face': a fully glazed elevation stretches over its entire width. On first glance the house appears to be a totally new structure; it is only on closer inspection that one becomes aware of the inner core. Although the volume of accommodation has actually been doubled, the architects nevertheless managed to argue their case to the planners that the original house has been retained intact; this is very clearly a house-within-a-house.

Throughout the house, there is great inventiveness in dealing with issues of flexibility of space and privacy. Zoning and cleverly concealed doors enable the house to be used in a variety of ways. It is evident that the architects had a very close relationship with the clients. Most of the joinery work is not only well designed and executed, it is also obviously the result of an extremely precise understanding of the clients' needs and desires. Overall the building is immaculately detailed and constructed. High-quality materials have been used discreetly to provide a neutral container for furnishings and artworks.

The front courtyard has been beautifully paved and planted. The landscaping here and in the rear garden was done by Dan Pearson in conjunction with sculptor William Pye.

The Lawns is an exemplar of how the twenty-first-century house can be incorporated into historic conservation areas as part of the continuing evolution of domestic architecture. It should also inspire other clients and architects to confront the challenges of the UK planning process.

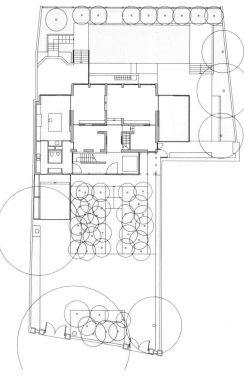

GROUND-FLOOR PLAN

TOP One of two remarkable first buildings on the 2001 shortlist (see also The Surgery, pages 140–41), this house-within-a-house provides a perfect example of how to play the planners at their own game.

OPPOSITE By wrapping the old house in glass, the architects have doubled the accommodation.

CLIENTS Frances and John Sorrell **STRUCTURAL ENGINEER** Arup **CONTRACTOR** Bradford Watts **CONTRACT VALUE** £1.1 million **PHOTOGRAPHER** Chris Gascoigne – VIEW

NATIONAL PORTRAIT GALLERY EXTENSION
.LONDON WC1 .JEREMY DIXON.EDWARD JONES

The National Portrait Gallery struggled with its Victorian inheritance to attract the visitors its superlative collections deserve. It had the air of a poor, shabby relation to its neighbour, the National Gallery. Now it has risen – via its spectacular new escalator – phoenix-like from the ashes of underachievement and, thanks in no small part to its fine new roof-top café, it is packing in the visitors.

The Oondatje Wing was the result of a deal between the National Portrait Gallery and the National Gallery to make use of a hidden courtyard between the two, to rework the circulation route for the NPG, and to add two new galleries, a lecture theatre and a public roof-top restaurant, thus by-passing the twentieth century in terms of gallery provision, and leaping directly into the twenty-first. Daylight carves its way to the ground floor, bouncing off the white walls and illuminating the entrance hall as the escalator draws visitors up towards the source of that light. The whole is supported on a single visible column, with the first-floor gallery appearing to hang in space. The views from the restaurant are, appropriately, of the temples to politics,

art and religion, the chief exponents of which grace the walls of the gallery.

Dixon.Jones realized that the key to unlocking the full potential of Ewan Christian's National Portrait Gallery, which, unusually, is stacked up on several floors, was to build an escalator that took visitors up to the top of the museum and then allowed them to percolate down. The architects have used the new-found space to transform a problematic Victorian gallery, revolutionizing its circulation and adding new galleries and the ancillary spaces that museums now need, all on land that only the architects saw could be used. The result is a model of the way Victorian museums can be brought up to modern standards.

Hidden from the street and entered through the Victorian inheritance, the spacious top-lit circulation hall has a cool majesty, and the ease with which visitors are drawn up through the building is impressive. The detailing and use of materials are immaculate throughout, highly functional and subservient to the displayed artworks. The building is uplifting and a joy to move around.

BELOW The axonometric shows how the architects have dropped the new accommodation into the light well between the two galleries.

RIGHT AND OPPOSITE Dixon.Jones's work provides an object lesson in how to drag a nineteenth-century building into the twenty-first century, rather in the way that Future Systems' Media Centre did at Lord's in 1999.

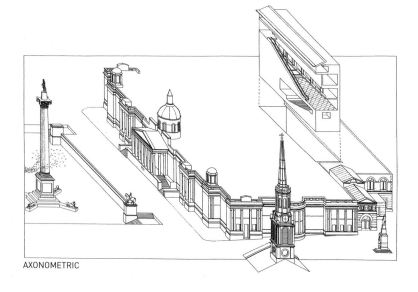

AXONOMETRIC

CLIENT National Portrait Gallery **STRUCTURAL, M&E AND ACOUSTIC ENGINEER** Arup
CONTRACTOR Norwest Holst Construction **CONTRACT VALUE** £13.2 million
PHOTOGRAPHER Dennis Gilbert – VIEW

PORTCULLIS HOUSE AND WESTMINSTER UNDERGROUND STATION .LONDON SW1 .MICHAEL HOPKINS AND PARTNERS

Portcullis House: A space audit confirmed the legendary accommodation problems faced by MPs, some occupying windowless offices, some in Portakabins parked on roofs or in dark corners. The answer was a building with new offices for 210 MPs, set within an enlarged secure perimeter. Michael Hopkins's solution arranges these offices in a simple plan and section around a glazed court, of similar proportions to Westminster Hall. New select-committee rooms are provided with full broadcast capability at first-floor level. Durable materials were specified for a building with a planned life of two hundred years: sandstone, patinated bronze and English oak. The building is also designed to consume one-third of the energy of an equivalent air-conditioned office. Air is drawn through the chimneys, cooled by well-water and distributed through ducts. Most of the structure was prefabricated off site to ensure quality and speed of construction.

The combination of an exemplary public-transport facility and a major public building is a rare one. In this case, problems of logistics, construction, security, planning, conservation and heritage issues produced a brief of enormous complexity. The result provides a new public facility and a landmark of instant gravitas and utility. It is one of the very few significant public projects in the capital in recent years that is not an adaptation of or addition to an existing building; externally it has to hold its own with Norman Shaw next door, Pugin and Barry across the road and Ralph Knott's County Hall on the other side of the Thames.

The courtyard, with its much-lambasted but flourishing trees, works supremely well as a place for MPs and their guests to meet and conduct informal business. The constant references to the House of Commons in the omnipresent oak (a by-product of the Great Storm of 1987) and the green leather in the committee rooms and offices are visual reminders that one is not in a superior office block but in the Mother of Parliaments.

Westminster Underground station: The legislation enabling the Jubilee line allowed for the demolition of structurally unsound buildings on the site, provided that a worthy replacement could be commissioned. Hopkins's proposal involved six huge columns that would support the building above and allow for a 30-metre-deep cavern, sited above double-stacked Tubes lines, through which the escalators would criss-cross. Throughout construction the District line, which cuts diagonally across the site, had to be kept open.

The station impresses by the apparent simplicity with which the huge technical and operational challenges have been resolved into a unique and memorable architectural experience. The lighting, in combination with masses of people gliding in all directions through the space, evokes a sense of wonder and excitement at modern technology and its contribution to city life. This station demonstrates that travelling on the Tube need not be a claustrophobic and unpleasant experience, but can be joyful and uplifting.

CLIENTS Parliamentary Works Directorate/London Underground **STRUCTURAL AND CIVIL ENGINEERS** Arup/G. Maunsell & Partners **CONTRACTORS** Laing Management/Balfour Beatty AMEC **CONTRACT VALUES** £165 million/£20 million **PHOTOGRAPHERS** Richard Davies (Portcullis House)/E.C. Dixon for London Underground (Westminster station)

ABOVE To have paid homage successfully both to Barry's and Pugin's Palace of Westminster (above, left; to the left, seen from across the river) and to the Norman Shaw Building (to the right) is perhaps the architects' greatest achievement in Portcullis House (above, right).

OPPOSITE Below ground the constraints are more to do with plumbing than planning, but at Westminster they have created what is perhaps the finest, certainly the most dramatic, of the twelve Jubilee line extension stations.

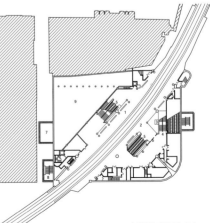

LEVEL 100 PLAN

THE SURGERY
.LONDON W6
.GUY GREENFIELD ARCHITECTS

Working, in effect, for three different clients – the health authority, the practice and the healthcare trust – the architects have produced a remarkably mature first building that responds to the clients' various needs and those of a planning authority that wanted a landmark for Hammersmith. The surgery lies hard by the Hammersmith flyover and shelters its occupants behind a curving white sculptural façade (reflecting the curve of the road overhead). The wall is made from a lightweight metal frame clad in Sto render. The roof and vertical walls are clad in copper. The single internal corridor on each floor provides further sound insulation for the doctors' rooms that overlook a secluded and remarkably peaceful (though sadly little-used) courtyard. This curtain-wall elevation uses a standard Crittall system. Internally, floors are of a stylish and durable Cumbrian slate.

Most acclaimed buildings have a good start in life: money (from popes to the Lottery), inspiring briefs (from museums to one-off houses) and, often, a stimulating context (from cliff sides to riverbanks). Good architects are then able to mix these heady ingredients and create something extraordinary. The Hammersmith surgery started with none of these cosseting benefits. It had a standard NHS budget and a standard NHS brief, and it is situated in a context that borders on the aggressive. The triumph of the architects and their exceptionally supportive clients is to have produced a building that transcends all these limitations.

The response to the problems of context is spot on: don't fight it or hide from it, but charm it with a sculptural form. The curved white sails work best at night but are not just a successful aesthetic device for the outside. Inside, they usher light into the corridors serving the medical rooms; corridors, so often the most disheartening moments in such buildings, are here genuinely life-affirming as they shape the light and allow limited glimpses out. The medical rooms themselves have an unexpected calmness, sheltered as they are from the traffic and overlooking a private courtyard.

The building is extraordinary in the real sense of the word; it creates something extra over and above the ordinary from an unpromising set of circumstances. The Hammersmith surgery is a shining example of the way that good architecture can and should operate at all levels of society. The judges claimed to have felt better when they left than when they arrived – and that is a good sign for a doctor's surgery.

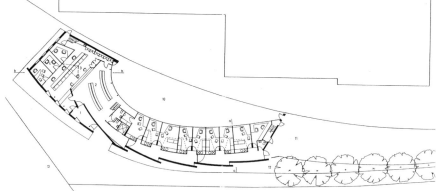

GROUND-FLOOR PLAN

TOP The corridor, instead of being a cramped architectural non-space, is the most uplifting space of all.

OPPOSITE The Surgery is a small but telling billboard advertising the power of good architecture to frazzled commuters on or beneath the Hammersmith flyover.

CLIENT West London Health Estates STRUCTURAL ENGINEER Cooper Associates CONTRACTOR Benson CONTRACT VALUE £1.16 million PHOTOGRAPHER Paul Tyagi – VIEW

THE STIRLING PRIZE 2001
.ISABEL ALLEN
EDITOR OF *THE ARCHITECTS' JOURNAL*

Stirling 2001 is remembered as much for the buildings that didn't win as for the building that did. There was Tate Modern, the spectre at the feast. Having opened with a great fanfare and to (almost) universal critical and popular acclaim, it was an obvious contender for the ultimate accolade but for the fact that, as non-RIBA members, Herzog and de Meuron were not eligible to enter any of its awards. (The practice subsequently got its paperwork in order just in time to clinch the Stirling Prize for its Laban dance centre in Deptford Creek in 2003.) Tate Modern's consequent absence from the Stirling shortlist was talked about almost as much as the shortlisted buildings themselves.

Then there was Westminster station, the most beautiful of the stations on the newly completed extension to the Jubilee line, and Portcullis House under which it sat. They did make it to the shortlist, but ultimately suffered from Michael Hopkins and Partners' decision to submit the two projects as a single entry. As Will Alsop, who was on the jury, put it: "I am pretty sure that if Hopkins had entered just Westminster Underground station without the ponderous building on top of it, it would have won."

And then there was Eden. A clear favourite with the bookies, the profession and the public, the Eden Project, more than any other building in the history of the Stirling Prize, seemed to be a dead cert. It had everything: rural regeneration, engineering miracles, ecological credentials and an instant reputation as the destination *du jour*. Everything, except the casting vote.

When the winner was announced on the night of the Stirling Prize dinner in the Great Court of the British Museum there was a palpable sense of amazement, not least from the newly anointed winner, Wilkinson Eyre. It was not that anybody doubted that the practice was a worthy Stirling Prize winner, it was simply that nobody would have predicted that Magna, for all its obvious merit, would be singled out as the practice's most significant triumph.

Chris Wilkinson gamely declared that Magna's "poetic combination of design and function" marked "a step forward in the firm's approach to architecture". But in truth it was much less of a milestone in the practice's career than, say, the enormous but surprisingly elegant Stratford Market depot, which had been passed over a few years before, or a number of truly ground-breaking bridge designs. When the practice picked up a second Stirling Prize for Gateshead Millennium Bridge in 2002 there was a much greater sense of justice having been done.

With the benefit of hindsight, Magna seems like a more obvious choice. It was very much of its time, a product of the Lottery-fuelled evangelism that preached that the Bilbao effect could be reproduced *ad infinitum*, that the gratuitous pursuit of the wow factor would not only pay for itself in visitor revenue but would also deliver the ultimate social good – regeneration. Now, of course, it all seems a little odd that anybody ever thought it was a good idea to put a pop museum in Sheffield or an earth museum in Doncaster. But at the time it all made perfect sense. What Rotherham needed was a science adventure centre. Indeed, it was hard to see how it had managed without one for quite so long.

And of the wave of Lottery projects that washed over the country in the space of a few mad Millennium years, Magna was clearly in the premier league. The raw material – a redundant steelworks – made it seem 'real', and the very fact that it breathed new life into dead space made it instantly less arbitrary and wilful than many of its new-build counterparts. In the scale of its vision, and the zestful dialogue between contemporary insertions and industrial grit, it had a certain spiritual kinship with that holy of holies, Tate Modern. As a nation, we had learned to confront our industrial past with a new maturity; to find delight and inspiration in structures that had previously been allowed to stagnate.

And Magna worked. As Alsop put it: "You can park near the building. At Eden, you have to park and then take a bus." Not perhaps the most elevated piece of architectural criticism, but an observation in the spirit of the small boy in the fairytale 'The Emperor's New Clothes'.

Eden didn't always work. In terms of sheer imaginative vision, and as an architectural and engineering achievement, it is astonishing indeed. The photographs that began to emerge from some hitherto neglected depths of Cornwall were greeted like images of the moon; some of them – with their strange curves, translucent textures and eerie shadows – looked as if they actually were. Other photographs, with their improbable groupings of over-scaled plants, evoked the possibility of an alien jungle sprouting up in some forgotten corner of our green and pleasant land. But by the time the Stirling jury came to visit, Eden had, to a certain extent, been a victim of its own success. Not only did you have to park and take the bus; more often than not you had to queue to park to take the bus. By the time you finally arrived you were ready for a cup of tea. The visitor experience was about traffic jams and cafés as much as spectacular biomes – a far cry from the near out-of-body sensation experienced by the clutch of architectural critics who made the pilgrimage to Eden before it officially opened its doors.

Magna was approached with fewer expectations, and managed to deliver more. Jury member Paul Finch, of *The Architects' Journal*, reported that the judges were "particularly impressed with the seamless integration between lighting, architecture, and exhibition design". But in the end, it was probably the feel-good factor that clinched it. After all, this was a determinedly populist panel. Alsop and Finch were joined by Marco Goldschmied, the party-going past-president of the RIBA, Janet 'Yoof TV' Street-Porter, and Alice Rawsthorn, who has since shocked her board of directors (and increased her visitor numbers) by bringing an exhibition on flower arranging to the Design Museum.

Without any sense of earnestness, Magna captured the *Zeitgeist* and delivered a great day out. It may even prove to have longevity. While the Pop Music Centre and the Earth Centre are now distant memories, Magna is still going strong.

2002

.JUDGES

Paul Hyett RIBA president (chair)

Paul Finch Publisher of *The Architects' Journal*

Wayne Hemingway Designer

Kate Mosse Novelist

Farshid Moussavi Architect

.THE STIRLING PRIZE WINNER

.THE STIRLING PRIZE SHORTLIST

.THE STIRLING PRIZE 2002

GATESHEAD MILLENNIUM BRIDGE
.GATESHEAD, TYNE AND WEAR
.WILKINSON EYRE ARCHITECTS

In 1997 Wilkinson Eyre – winner of the 2001 Stirling Prize for Magna, the Science Adventure Centre in Rotherham – won a competition to design a new foot-and-cycle crossing of the Tyne to link Gateshead with Newcastle. The crossing was to play a pivotal role in the regeneration of Gateshead, along with Antony Gormley's *Angel of the North*, which kick-started the Bilbao effect on the south bank of the Tyne, Ellis Williams's Baltic, the centre for contemporary art, and Foster and Partners' Sage music centre. The bridge ties this new arts hub to Newcastle's recently developed Quayside and was crucial to Gateshead being voted RIBA/Arts Council England Client of the Year in 2005.

Contrary to popular misconception, this is Gateshead's bridge, not Newcastle's, thanks to a complete lack of support from the city of Newcastle, summed up in the attitude, "If they wanna come over here, let 'em build their own bridge. Why would we wanna gan over there?" In fact, increasingly, the people of Newcastle might want to do just that, because Gateshead, once merely a gateway to Newcastle, is becoming a destination in its own right. Anyway, Gateshead has built its own bridge, and – look closely – it doesn't even land on Newcastle soil but on a pier loosely attached to the north bank. The clients, inspirational council leader Mick Henry and city engineer John Johnson, are to be congratulated on their restraint in not dubbing it 'Not the Newcastle Bridge' or even the 'Bridge to Nowhere'.

The brief called for a footbridge that met the ground on either riverbank; other bridges, because of the Tyne's steep gorge, do so further inland. This was likely to mean a steep gradient (or steps) if there was to be sufficient clearance even for small craft, making the bridge inaccessible to wheelchair users or any but the fittest cyclists. Wilkinson Eyre instead proposed a curved deck to reduce the gradient. This in turn suggested a solution to the other part of the brief: a mechanism for allowing the occasional passage of bigger traffic, for example, the tall ships. The Swing Bridge, some way up stream, is a low-level solution, but that pivots from an island. The Victorian Tyne Bridge solves the obstruction to shipping problem by towering high above the water. When it is in its lowered position, Wilkinson Eyre's bridge allows the same clearance as the Swing Bridge; when raised it gives a 25-metre clearance, the same as the massive Tyne Bridge. And it does so in spectacular fashion.

The idea is eminently simple: a pair of arches – one *is* the deck, the other supports the deck. Both arches pivot around their common springing point, allowing shipping to pass beneath. As the whole bridge tilts it undergoes a metamorphosis into a grand arch in an operation that evokes the slow opening of a huge eye.

PAGES 146–47 AND ABOVE Seldom if ever has there been so little disparity between conception and execution. By night or by day, this perfectly realized piece of architecture and engineering lifts the spirits of all who see and use it.

OPPOSITE Jim Eyre's sketches show clearances with the bridge in the lowered (top) and raised (centre) positions, and the tilt mechanism (bottom).

CLIENT Gateshead Council **STRUCTURAL AND M&E ENGINEER** Gifford and Partners **LIGHTING CONSULTANT** Jonathan Speirs & Associates **CONTRACTOR** Harbour & General **CONTRACT VALUE** £17.7 million **PHOTOGRAPHER** Graeme Peacock

The design is a subtle mix of the robust and the delicate and contrasts effectively with the vast bulk of Baltic, which it abuts. The bridge spans 105 metres between two caissons, each housing a public viewing deck. An all-glass pavilion encloses the plant and hydraulics on the south bank. The parabolic arch has a kite-shaped cross-section that tapers in plan and elevation. The pedestrian route is slightly raised above the cycleway and there is intermittent screening. Seats give the bridge a sense of place as well as of purpose.

The structure was built in sections in Bolton, assembled at Wallsend, then shipped upstream and dropped into place – to within a tolerance of one millimetre – on its concrete abutments by a giant crane. One false move could have wiped out the thousands of people watching the procedure on both banks.

The original judges were not fortunate enough to see the bridge raised but said they could imagine the drama created when it opens to allow watercraft to pass underneath. They concluded that the engineering challenge was immense, and the solution innovative, bold and engaging — in short, really outstanding. The Stirling judges were luckier: Gateshead engineer John Johnson allowed Paul Hyett, the RIBA president, to press the button to raise the bridge. In choosing the bridge as the winner, the judges described it as architecture and engineering in close harmony. Few pieces of architecture have had such a powerful social effect, providing a stimulus to regeneration and helping end the traditional enmity between Gateshead and Newcastle, even bringing the cities together to mount a joint, though ultimately unsuccessful, bid for European Capital of Culture in 2008. The bridge is, the judges concluded, a new icon, the one truly memorable piece of architecture in 2002. Overall, they thought Wilkinson Eyre's was the obvious solution to the problem set by the brief of how to build a bridge that meets the ground but also allows shipping to pass: it was just that no one had ever thought of it before.

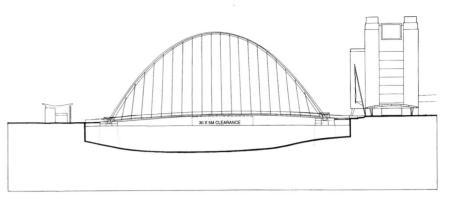

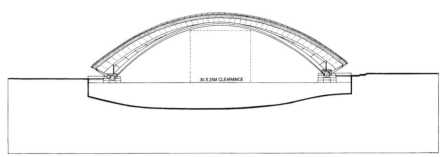

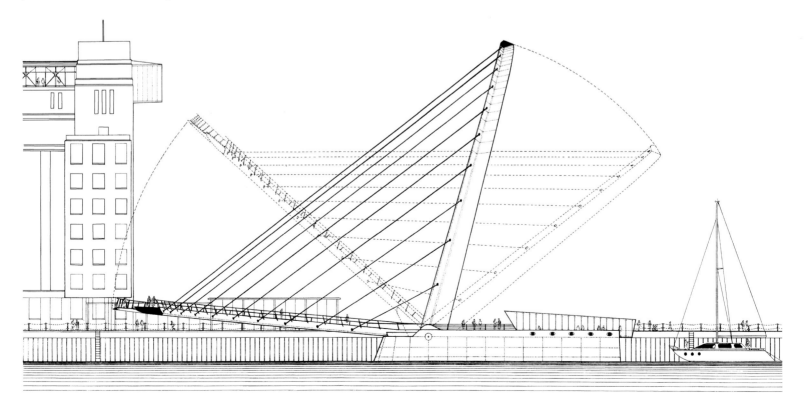

DANCE BASE .EDINBURGH .MALCOLM FRASER ARCHITECTS

WINNER OF THE ADAPT TRUST ACCESS AWARD

Dance Base is one of the most complex projects to win an RIBA Award in recent years and a remarkable challenge in terms of access. Constructed on the lower slopes of the volcanic crag topped by Edinburgh Castle, behind and above existing buildings, it provides a group of four excellent dance studios. Few planning authorities would have been so bold as to risk so striking a new building in such a context, and the authority in this case is to be commended for its daring.

Arranged over a succession of four levels (each of which is accessible by a combination of lifts, stairs and ramps), the building magically exploits the topography of the site. From the Grassmarket it is hardly noticeable: there is a little-altered shopfront and an entrance to a close (like so many others in this city), leading to a generous reception space. From here a ramp climbs gently, hugging an illuminated original stone wall, to a second foyer and coffee area, where the high-quality concrete is exposed.

Each dance studio is unique. One, converted from an existing building, is a simple space with a steel-trussed roof and a single roof light punched through to offer a dramatic view of the castle. A second, like a giant conservatory, has an almost entirely glazed roof. The castle's looming presence seems to fill the space entirely. This studio, opening off the foyer, is used by Dance Base's integrated creative-movement programme for dancers with disabilities, who often work with their carers. The third has a floating steel roof suspended above its perimeter walls. And the last studio, the most restrained, is enclosed by a powerful *in situ* concrete structure centrally planned on the space below. At the top of the building the space opens out on to a series of terraces and gardens, colonizing the existing hillside and providing a wonderful amenity in this dense, urban location.

To have made an accessible building on such a steep site is no mean achievement. At a time when more and more people with disabilities are asserting their rights to active, fulfilling lives, Dance Base provides ample opportunities. Physical access has been provided throughout, but it is in the design detail that the building is particularly successful: the use of colour, good signage and hearing-assistive systems make it a joy for people with sensory impairments to use as well.

This is a building that makes you want to dance even if you can't; an inspiring building, much loved by the professional and amateur dancers who make excellent use of its facilities. To dance, to choreograph, to teach and to learn here must be an endless pleasure. It is also, plainly, the work of a local architect who knows and loves his city and has been determined to make a lasting and significant contribution to its townscape.

ABOVE Dance Base is scarcely noticeable from the historic Grassmarket (top), yet the old building provides a light and airy dance studio on its top floor.

OPPOSITE The building climbs the crags of Castle Rock, providing views to inspire dancers and choreographers.

CLIENT Dance Base **STRUCTURAL ENGINEER** Cundall Johnston and Partners
THEATRE DESIGNER Andrew Storer Designs **CONTRACTOR** HBG Construction
CONTRACT VALUE £5 million **PHOTOGRAPHER** Keith Hunter

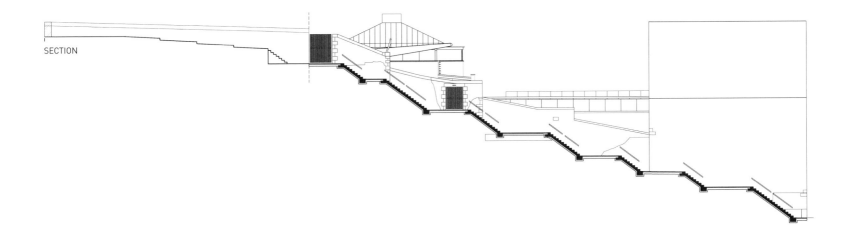

SECTION

DOWNLAND GRIDSHELL, WEALD AND DOWNLAND OPEN AIR MUSEUM .CHICHESTER, WEST SUSSEX .EDWARD CULLINAN ARCHITECTS

The context is as extraordinary as the building, which in itself is the first permanent timber-gridshell building in the world. The Weald and Downland Open Air Museum is an admirable institution that presents the history of vernacular architecture in the south-east of England in a hugely enjoyable way and on a lovely site. The museum has been responsible for saving many historic buildings threatened with destruction by development and has formed important collections of materials and artefacts. Under the directorships of the late Chris Zeuner and, latterly, Richard Harris, it has been a potent source for the teaching of craft building techniques.

Rather than construct a fake barn to house the storage and workshop space it needed, the museum decided to commission a new work of architecture that would reflect the relevance of the vernacular tradition today. The conservation workshop, where buildings are brought and worked on before being returned to site, is 50 metres long and sits above a concrete plinth that houses offices and storage. The structure is like a fine musical instrument, and uses a variety of different woods best suited to purpose: local or Normandy oak, ash, Douglas fir and Western red cedar. Wherever possible, the timber laths with which the gridshell is constructed are the natural, renewable product of woodland management. They are used here in a highly innovative way, although there are antecedents, outside the construction process, in the design of World War II aircraft. The design process,

inspired by Royal Gold medallist Frei Otto and carried out in close collaboration with engineer Buro Happold, achieved sublime results that are far more than functional, although the building has all the toughness and adaptability demanded by the brief. The construction process presented a huge challenge to the contractor and to other specialists, as the computer-designed shell was fabricated by hand. The project fostered creativity and exceptional craftsmanship.

This was as 'modern' a building as any the jury visited, one where brief, process, construction, materials and detail all combine to produce a whole that is much more than the sum of the parts. The Heritage Lottery Fund, part-financier of the project, has since used it as an example of a model procurement method for future schemes in which it is involved.

The museum is ground-breaking, lovable and a joy to visit. In truth it is a functional structure, but it has transcended this role to become an educational, social and community space. It is a major work by a practice that has enriched the architectural culture of Britain over four decades. The building is inclusive, accessible, innovative and (truly) sustainable.

The Stirling judges thought the gridshell shows that good design does make a difference and demonstrates what can happen when a gifted architect remains closely involved throughout the process. The gridshell, they concluded, is a thing of beauty inside and out and a tribute to all who worked on it.

EAST ELEVATION 1:100

CROSS SECTION 1:100

WEST ELEVATION 1:100

ELEVATIONS, SECTION AND SITE PLAN

RIGHT Ted Cullinan's gridshell perfectly practises what it preaches; it is a green building, the purpose of which is to demonstrate the recycling of old buildings.

OPPOSITE The Frei Otto-inspired gridshell, with its sinuous timber frame, appears to grow out of its woodland setting. In many years this would have walked away with the Stirling Prize.

CLIENT Weald and Downland Open Air Museum
STRUCTURAL AND M&E ENGINEER Buro Happold **CONTRACTOR** E.A. Chiverton
CONTRACT VALUE £1.6 million **PHOTOGRAPHER** Stuart Keegan

ERNSTING'S SERVICE CENTRE
.COESFELD-LETTE, GERMANY
.DAVID CHIPPERFIELD ARCHITECTS

This scheme represents another successful German commission for David Chipperfield. Ernsting is a clothing retailer, and the vivid examples of its children's range provide a bizarre contrast with the grey coolness of the building that contains them. But the juxtaposition is not unique: an enthusiast for Modernism, the client, Kurt Ernsting, has already had Bruno Reichlin, Fabio Reinhart and Santiago Calatrava design parts of the site for him. This is clearly a man who collects good buildings like other well-off people collect cars or paintings. Although these were all good pieces of architecture in their own right (in particular, Calatrava's bridge), the site as a whole did not have a clear identity. The challenge laid down in the competition brief was not only to add another fine piece of architecture, but to create a sense of campus and to unify the spaces between existing and new buildings.

Chipperfield's winning entry proposed a pavilion of open and flexible office spaces arranged around a series of gardens, courtyards and an atrium that acts as a generous space in which employees can meet and interact. Within the offices, workspaces are transparent and humane, taking full advantage of the parkland setting. Although open-plan, each workspace has its own balcony, where elegant sunscreens provide protection from the sun. This standard of office provision is almost unthinkable in the United Kingdom.

From first sight, the service centre exudes the confidence of a high-quality corporate headquarters. However, closer inspection reveals that this building rises way above the norm. What is really impressive is the variety of spaces, views and connections that the architects have conjured out of an apparently simple plan, based on a repeated module. The architects have used real skill in exploiting a luxurious budget. The result is a remarkably generous set of spaces, with high ceilings, wide corridors and open loggias.

The mastery is in the deployment of those elements and their control through the established virtues of clarity and attention to proportion. The resulting building is both calm and calming and has a timeless quality. Particularly impressive are the controlled framing of views to the outside and the handling of light in the main spaces (this must be one of the more enviable staff canteens anywhere). All of this is conjured up from a limited palette of materials that, in other hands, might have been unforgiving, but here are made almost soft and certainly human by their handling.

The Stirling judges praised the centre for its maturity and control. They enjoyed the almost surreal juxtaposition of the client's populist clothing range with the high art of the architecture. Good architecture should lift the spirits, and this building does that very well. What is more, the building's calming effect has led to an increase in productivity, which is no mean feat.

ABOVE David Chipperfield's super-rational, super-cool exteriors and interiors have given a demanding client everything he wanted and a little more he never knew he wanted.

OPPOSITE Despite the simple, repeated geometry, Chipperfield has produced a variety of spaces, connections and perspectives.

CLIENT Ernsting STRUCTURAL ENGINEERS Jane Wernick Associates/Arup Düsseldorf
CONTRACTOR E. Heitkamp CONTRACT VALUE £11.5 million PHOTOGRAPHERS Christian Richters (above; opposite bottom)/Edmund Sumner – VIEW (opposite top)

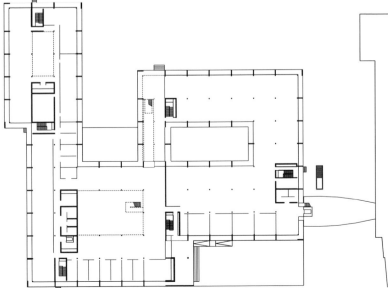

GROUND-FLOOR PLAN

HAMPDEN GURNEY CHURCH OF ENGLAND PRIMARY SCHOOL .LONDON W1 .BUILDING DESIGN PARTNERSHIP

The new Hampden Gurney School stands on a site previously occupied by one- and two-storey buildings on a World War II bombsite. The previous building had reached the end of its useful life. The school, which prides itself on its high academic standards, had sought for a number of years to improve its premises. The solution came through a deal with the contractor Jarvis, which wanted to use part of the site for housing. The new building turns school design on its head, and turns heads too.

The new building makes the school the cornerpiece of a re-created Marylebone city block that looks out towards the constant activity of the nearby Edgware Road. The building, located on the prominent south-west corner, forms an internal courtyard with two new inter-related residential street buildings. This provides the school with the best aspect for sunlight, and the six levels of the building give it prominence within the neighbourhood. The 'vertical school' offers opportunities for safe, weatherproof play in the open-air play decks and the prospect of open-air classrooms on warm days, with good north light in the teaching areas. Not only do Hampden Gurney's children move up the school metaphorically as they get older, they also do so literally in terms of classroom occupation of the floors.

The school has a steel frame crowned with an arched truss at fourth-floor level; Macalloy bars support the bridge steels in the light well, transferring the loads to the truss overhead and enabling the communal hall to be free of columns. The outer envelope is brick, chosen to be sympathetic to the surrounding London stock-brick buildings, while the curve of the playdecks is formed by the 1.9-metre glass balustrading supported on planar-fixed steel uprights. A tensile roof springs from the steel truss, protecting the light well below and creating threshold spaces on the roof play area.

As befits such an innovative multistorey primary school developed on an inner-city site, the planning is highly creative. There is a covered playground on each level shared between three classrooms, allowing the children to play even when it is raining. A central atrium brings light into the centre of the building, and the overall organization and environment feel safe and spacious.

The Stirling judges were moved to see the obvious pride on the children's faces, and they were impressed by the way the architects have thrown the rule book inspired by Hampshire County Council out of the sixth-floor window and invented a new form. This form takes its precedents from the Victorian school and will hopefully itself prove to be a precedent that will develop and mature in other hands and on other sites.

ABOVE The multipurpose hall on the lower ground floor benefits from natural light brought in by the central atrium.

OPPOSITE The tight inner-city site suggested its own solution: a multistorey, shiny public façade all but filling the available site, but with ample play areas on the decks and roof.

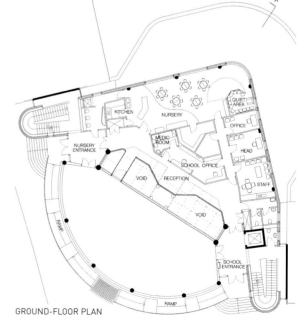

GROUND-FLOOR PLAN

CLIENT Hampden Gurney School STRUCTURAL AND M&E ENGINEER Building Design Partnership CONTRACTOR Jarvis Construction (UK) CONTRACT VALUE £6 million PHOTOGRAPHER Martine Hamilton Knight

156

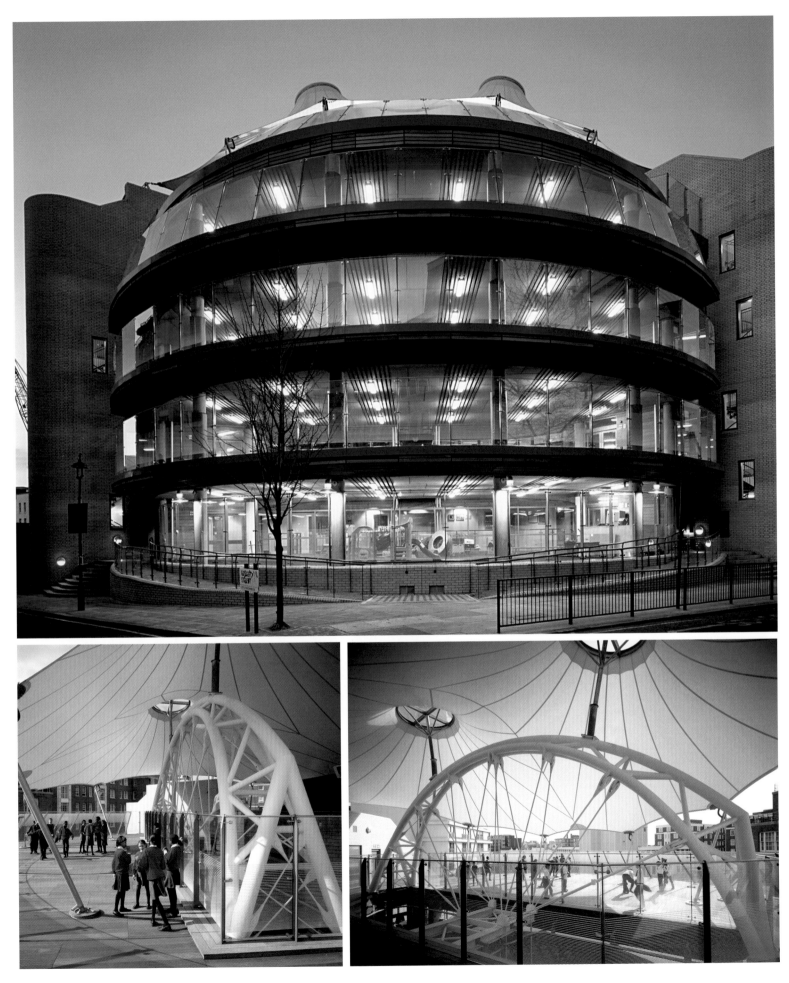

LLOYD'S REGISTER OF SHIPPING
.LONDON EC3
.RICHARD ROGERS PARTNERSHIP

Out of adversity and conflict often comes good architecture. Basil Spence's Coventry Cathedral used the blackened shell of the firebombed medieval church as its inspiration and its pivot. Richard Rogers Partnership's new headquarters for Lloyd's Register of Shipping does much the same thing, combining the reworking of existing listed properties with the insertion of an uncompromising new structure. The project develops, refines and updates the trademark elemental construction language seen at Lloyd's nearby sister building to create a vibrant and animated presence within the City of London.

From street level the new building is generally concealed by the surrounding original buildings, its presence only revealed through an abstract louvred elevation to Fenchurch Street and glimpses across a small courtyard to the main entrance. In longer views, however, the new building can be clearly seen, its slender glass lift towers growing out of the site to soar above the enclosing stone façades. This is a mature work by a mature practice, and the hand of architect Graham Stirk is much in evidence.

The project rationalizes the original disparate mix of buildings and levels into a coherent group linked at first-floor level. The need to retain a churchyard within the site has been turned to an advantage, creating an intimate entrance court, a calm space through which workers pass to reach the new building.

The first of two full-height atria soars above the entrance space, allowing visitors to see the different levels within the building. On an operational level, the atria break up what could have been a bland expanse of office floorplates, allowing daylight to filter through to the workstations and creating a means of mediating the temperature differences between the outside and the offices. Energy efficiency is explored throughout the design, which incorporates such mechanisms as chilled beams and louvred façade systems to respond to external environmental conditions, and so minimize running costs and create comfortable working environments.

The quality of the working environment is continued through the attention to detail in both the new building and the refurbishment of the original premises. The articulation of the new build creates an identity and character within the offices and emphasizes the kit-like method of construction that was necessary because of difficult access to the confined site.

The Stirling judges commended the way in which the building overcomes planning and site constraints to add a very special piece of architecture to the City. They described it as a thoroughly exciting building in a difficult context: high-tech guts dropped into an existing landscape, with all the services pared down into fragile elements. They particularly enjoyed the urban space of the courtyard, formerly the churchyard, which gives the building a popular outdoor foyer.

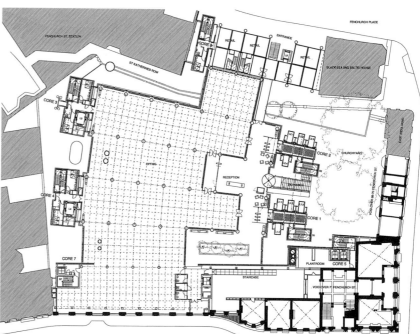

GROUND-FLOOR PLAN

CLIENT Lloyd's Register of Shipping **STRUCTURAL ENGINEER** Anthony Hunt Associates **CONTRACTOR** Sir Robert McAlpine **CONTRACT VALUE** £70 million **PHOTOGRAPHERS** Dennis Gilbert – VIEW (above)/Katsuhisa Kida (opposite)

TOP The complexity of the project is shown by the plan: the architects have had to work with a number of existing buildings around a retained churchyard.

ABOVE AND OPPOSITE The new-build elements – up to fourteen storeys – are uncompromising yet are all but hidden at street level.

MILLENNIUM WING, NATIONAL GALLERY OF IRELAND .DUBLIN, IRELAND .BENSON + FORSYTH

Although the façade on Lincoln Place contains many clues as to what to expect inside, nothing quite prepares you for the majesty of the soaring entrance hall. Here, in the Millennium Wing of the National Gallery of Ireland in Dublin, Benson + Forsyth has taken the experience of working on the Museum of Scotland and refined and honed it to produce these breathtaking gallery spaces. It is a glowing cathedral of a place, combining loftiness with intimacy, gravity with playfulness, and theatricality with calmness. It triumphantly fulfils the client's brief that it "should be dignified and expressive of its time and its function. ... The interior should be legible to visitors and a delight to experience."

The Millennium Wing was the result of an international competition won in 1996. It finally opened to the public in 2002 after many setbacks. These resulted in a reduction in gallery space and the inclusion within the footprint of two existing buildings, one Georgian and one Regency. Nonetheless, the completed gallery, far from feeling like a compromise, has a sense of inevitability about it. Handled by less-confident architects, the retained elements might have wrecked the purity of the scheme; here Benson + Forsyth has made a merit out of the planners' necessity and created a space (used as the café) that is playful and respectful to the city's past.

The new gallery is linked to the existing one at right angles and has its own street frontage, which is treated as a play of shifting planes of Portland stone between which the inside of the gallery can be glimpsed. Articulation with the city continues throughout the building, culminating at roof level, where it takes its place within a roof-top world from which the familiar landmarks of Dublin can be seen.

What gives this building its very special timeless quality is its consistency, which extends into its detailing. A special mention should be made of the use throughout of a light stone-coloured self-finished plaster that seems to absorb light and radiate it back again.

The Stirling judges enjoyed themselves here, even at the end of a day of visits taking in three countries. Dubliners can count themselves lucky that they can enjoy such a fine addition to their National Gallery on a regular basis. Although the vast vertical circulation spaces are asymmetrical and sometimes dizzying, the galleries themselves are ordered and calm, allowing visitors to concentrate on the paintings they have come to see. Curatorial demands are not so stringent as to exclude natural daylight, so there are very few areas that are artificially lit, and this adds to the accessibility of the experience. The extension has given the museum a new space, new life and a sense of drama that permeates the building from entrance hall to roof-top.

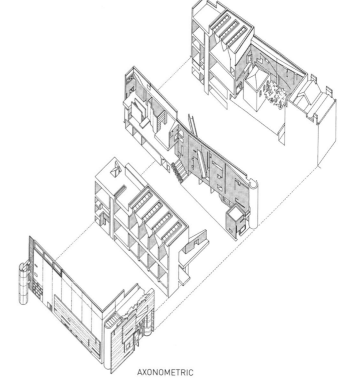

AXONOMETRIC

CLIENT The National Gallery of Ireland STRUCTURAL ENGINEER O'Connor Sutton Cronin CONTRACTOR Michael McNamara & Co. CONTRACT VALUE £10.7 million PHOTOGRAPHER Hélène Binet

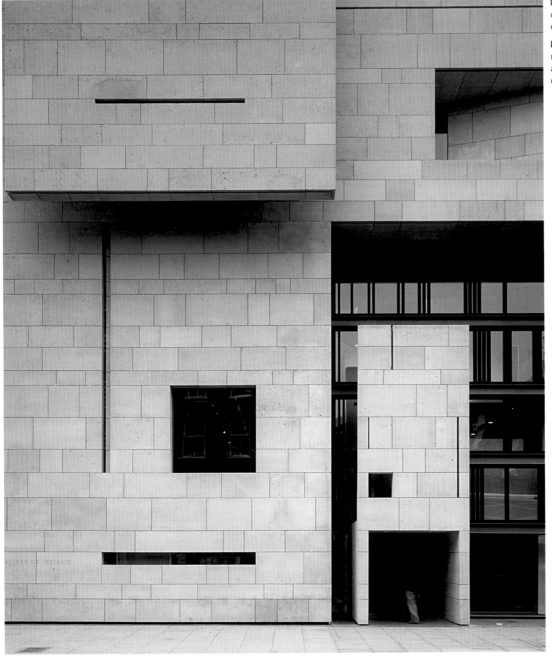

OPPOSITE The shifting planes of Portland stone on the Lincoln Place façade allow only glimpses of the cathedral-like interiors.

LEFT AND BELOW Benson + Forsyth has honed and refined its work on the Museum of Scotland, creating a more mature building that still retains a similar degree of intrigue and excitement.

THE STIRLING PRIZE 2002
.GILES WORSLEY
ARCHITECTURE CRITIC OF *THE DAILY TELEGRAPH*

"But is it architecture?" That was the question the critics asked when the Stirling Prize went to Wilkinson Eyre's Gateshead Millennium Bridge, built with the engineers Gifford and Partners. The answer was that it might not be a building in a conventional sense, but it was certainly architecture. An elegant structure that perfectly married engineering and architecture, it represented the epitome of design for the high-tech generation. It was the hot favourite to win, and as judging on the day took place at the Baltic art gallery, overlooking the bridge, it had a strong psychological advantage.

The Gateshead Millennium Bridge was built to serve a practical purpose, linking the north and south banks of the Tyne, but its message was as much symbolic as practical. It was meant to show that after years of neglect the Tyneside fronts of Newcastle and Gateshead were back on the map. Wilkinson Eyre worked under two constraints, one practical, one psychological. The first was that the bridge had to be able to open to let occasional boats through. This it does with great showmanship, tilting slowly upwards and then settling back into place. The second was the relationship between the bridge and the iconic earlier bridges spanning the Tyne, particularly Mott, Hay & Anderson's New Tyne Road Bridge. Many designers would have been intimidated by these precedents. Wilkinson Eyre rose superbly to the challenge, presenting a design that echoes but does not mimic the New Tyne Road Bridge.

Beyond the Millennium Bridge the field seemed open. Richard Rogers came up with a typically slick scheme in the City of London, the Lloyd's Register of Shipping on Fenchurch Street. Here the demands of conservation pushed Rogers to produce one of his most interesting buildings. Because Fenchurch Street was a conservation area, Rogers was not allowed to knock down the buildings fronting the street. Nor could he build on the area immediately behind since it is a former churchyard. So he was forced to follow that very traditional city plan of an imposing building set back from the street behind a courtyard. In doing so he discovered, almost by default, how to fit a tall building of fourteen storeys into the City while retaining its street-level integrity. It is a lesson others would do well to heed. Sadly, the low ceiling heights of the offices inside made them distinctly depressing, which somewhat spoiled Rogers's chances.

The scheme that was least easily comprehensible from photographs was Malcolm Fraser's Dance Base in Edinburgh, which looked nothing until you visited it. Taking a complicated site rising up Castle Rock from the Grassmarket, the architect created four studios on three levels from a mix of existing and new spaces. It was a skilful piece of urban planning with impressively effective access, but at heart it was a conversion, and conversions seldom win the Stirling Prize. And certainly not two years running.

For architecture with a capital A, there were two very different schemes: David Chipperfield's service centre for Ernsting in Coesfeld-Lette, Germany, and Benson + Forsyth's Millennium Wing at the National Gallery of Ireland in Dublin.

Chipperfield's building had all the properties of a classic building. Unflawed and well built, it had the sense of being the creation of a master at work. Chipperfield's cool and restrained architecture was the antithesis of the showy, high-tech and weirdly shaped attention-seeking buildings that tend to capture public attention, but it represented an important and growing strand of British architecture. It would have been a worthy winner, but the sense that it could just as well be an art gallery as the headquarters of a cheap-clothing manufacturer and retailer;

that while it encapsulated what is attractive about Chipperfield's work, it did not really develop it; and, above all, the fact that it lacked obvious show-stopping appeal were all held against it.

Of all the buildings on the shortlist, Benson + Forsyth's Millennium Wing gave the greatest architectural thrill. This was raw architecture, the manipulation of light and space, mixed with a complex set of messages exploring the interaction between the building and the surrounding city. Its weakness lay in the fact that it worked best as a stand-alone building and did not really connect well with the older galleries that house most of the collection.

After the profound architectural tension of Chipperfield and Benson + Forsyth, BDP's Hampden Gurney primary school in Marylebone was a bit of a comedown. Indeed, some thought it sat rather uncomfortably on the shortlist. But although Hampden Gurney was not great architecture, of all the buildings on the shortlist it carried the strongest social message. This was an ingenious scheme that created a new model for urban schools, harking back to Victorian precedents by piling classrooms one above another while adding enclosed playing areas on each floor. It was the cleverest breakthrough in school design for a generation, and came at a time when the banality of new PFI-funded schools was causing despair, particularly in Scotland.

The most sensuous of the buildings on the shortlist, however, the one that many architects regretted did not win the prize, was Ted Cullinan's workshop at the Weald and Downland Open Air Museum. Cullinan and the engineer Buro Happold took timber, the most basic of materials, and used the latest computerized technology to create a building – a gridshell created out of thin slats of green oak – that was as structurally ingenious as anything being built today. Traditional and yet modern, poetic and yet as rigorously functional in its marriage of architecture and engineering as the Gateshead Millennium Bridge, the gridshell captured the imagination of all who visited it. In an age less fixated on the easy image and on the high-tech marriage of architecture and engineering it would probably have won. I still regret that it did not.

Note: Sadly, Giles Worsley died at the indecently early age of forty-four, shortly before this book went to press. This book is dedicated to his memory.

2003

.JUDGES

George Ferguson RIBA president (chair)

Isabel Allen Editor of *The Architects' Journal*

Julian Barnes Novelist

Justine Frischmann Singer and TV presenter

Chris Wilkinson Architect and Stirling Prize winner in 2001 and 2002

.THE STIRLING PRIZE WINNER

.THE STIRLING PRIZE SHORTLIST

.THE STIRLING PRIZE 2003

LABAN
.LONDON SE8
.HERZOG & DE MEURON

"Laban will do for dance what Tate Modern has done for art", announces a screen inside the entrance to this less grandiloquent but equally eloquent building by the Swiss pair Herzog & de Meuron. And it is true: there is a creative buzz about the place that hits you the moment you step inside the translucent polychromatic polycarbonate screen.

This was Herzog & de Meuron's first RIBA Awards entry. To win on a first outing is no mean achievement, but then this is no ordinary practice; it's one that will, over the years, mop up just about every award that is going.

Laban has given Deptford a significant and beautiful new landmark. The building is a singular and simple container with a double-skinned wall, the outer layer being polycarbonate, the inner one a utilitarian and economic layer of insulation and translucent glass panels. At carefully considered moments the inner and outer worlds are more immediately connected by ambiguously scaled, framed transparent panels. This compositional device is cleverly mirrored in the plan form, punctuated by spaces of various heights and shape related to their function. The rectangular plan is warped by the gentle curve that both welcomes the visitor and responds to the verticality of the nearby St Paul's Church.

The dance studios are pressed up against the external envelope and utilize the exquisite coloured translucency of the walls to separate the plane of the timber floors from the massive ribbed-concrete soffits; likewise, the position on plan of the library, workshops and offices. The labyrinthine quality of the internal circulation is dramatized by the high chroma of the wall paint, darkly toned interiors, the interior light wells and, most dramatically, the sculptural gloss-black-painted spiral stairs, one at the front, the other at the rear. The creative and inspiring world of dance is matched by that of art and architecture.

Inside the space there are ramps up towards studios and theatres or down towards the café and treatment centres. All the activities of the dance centre are intermixed and distributed on two levels, promoting communication throughout this complex building. Circulation takes the form of an H around the main theatre and is defined by the two light wells (a third was sadly lost to economies). Each of the eleven studios has a subtly different size, height, form and colour.

The architectural ambition and ideas of this building are realized at the highest level. The quality of light – both from the inside out and from the outside in – is exceptionally beautiful for the occupiers, visitors and neighbours. The coloured panels were devised in collaboration with artist Michael Craig-Martin. Being mounted in front of the glass, they serve as a protective

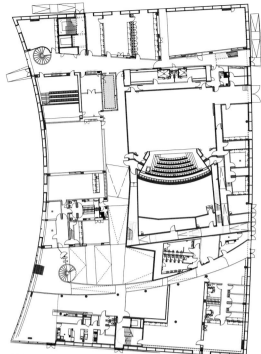

GROUND-FLOOR PLAN

CLIENT Laban STRUCTURAL AND M&E ENGINEER Whitbybird THEATRE CONSULTANT Carr & Angier CONTRACTOR Ballast Construction CONTRACT VALUE £14.4 million PHOTOGRAPHERS Dennis Gilbert – VIEW (right)/Merlin Hendy (pp. 166–67, main photo)/Merlin Hendy & Martin Rose (p. 167, bottom right; opposite)/Will Pryce (p. 167, top right)

sunshield and improve the building's energy efficiency, as well as being objects of beauty in their own right.

The building is inventive in the way its form reveals the choreography of movement. The public circulation spaces are full of wit in the curving handrail, which counters the hard line of the dance-studio bar. This is a project in which the design vision has been carried through from the first ideas to its completed detail. The extent of innovation in the project is apparent throughout but never shouted. It is a graceful building, generous in its relationship to its context: its reference to St Paul's Church is geometrically precise, while it is calmly haphazard alongside the meandering Deptford Creek.

The judges thought this to be an extraordinarily fine building, one that raises the expectations of architecture in its engagement both with art forms and with the local context. It makes a major contribution to the artistic life of the community while acting as a catalyst for the regeneration of the whole area.

Novelist Julian Barnes summed up the feelings of the Stirling jury: "It hits you straight between the eyes as soon as you get there. It has the same movement, youth, agility, pizzazz, front to it that its students have – it's very seductive. The immediate reaction of everyone in the bus as we arrived was to go, 'Wow!'"

PAGES 166–67 Laban is a clean, elegant and in many ways remarkably restrained landmark and symbol of the regeneration of Deptford.

OPPOSITE Internally, Laban has all the sinuous grace of a dancer: curving walls, twisting handrails, even pirouetting stairs.

BELOW By night the building glows, displaying the activity within as if it were back-projected on to the polycarbonate screen.

BEDZED
.WALLINGTON, SURREY .BILL DUNSTER ARCHITECTS
WINNER OF THE RIBA JOURNAL SUSTAINABILITY AWARD

BedZED is a twenty-first-century take on the English Garden City. Few schemes built in the United Kingdom over the last few years can be said to have genuinely moved on architectural knowledge and culture; BedZED is one.

The architects describe BedZED as the first large-scale "carbon-neutral" community in the United Kingdom. What they mean is that the architecture helps its residents cut carbon emissions from personal transport and emissions involved in bringing their food to the door, as well as those derived from running their homes. As such it is exemplary sustainable-housing design. Predicted energy savings are in the region of 60 per cent. Grey and black water are processed on site. The scheme employs a whole range of sustainable technologies. To achieve this in a one-off experimental house would have been good going; to do it in a publicly funded mixed-tenure housing scheme is quite astonishing. Even before a visit, expectations are therefore set high, although they are accompanied by the nagging doubt that one might be assaulted by hair-shirt worthiness.

However, all doubts are swept away by the sheer exuberance of the place, announced by the wind cowls nodding in the breeze like a herd of strange, multicoloured beasts. What is even more refreshing is that the innovations in sustainable design are accompanied by innovations in spatial design. The flats and houses are a delight to be in, full of light and incident. The use

of the sunspaces (generally double-height glazed areas) as an environmental buffer provides a whole range of variations in the way the accommodation is used throughout the year. The high density of the scheme does not lead to claustrophobia, mainly because clever manipulation in section gives a patch of private external space to each unit. Best of all are the sky gardens reached over bridges, which provide a sense of release and expansion. BedZED jolts one into revising the architectural value system, raising consciousness of a much wider set of issues than the niceties of a detail.

About 95 per cent of the structural steel was sourced within an average 56-kilometre radius of the site, mostly from Brighton station, which was being refurbished at the time. None of the steel was melted down; it was simply used as found, so that evidence of its original use can be seen in the houses. The architects even stopped the contractors grinding the steel down to make it look like new. Bill Dunster believes that most workaday buildings could use recycled steel in this way.

The aim at BedZED is not just to create sustainable housing and workspaces, but also to develop a new architectural language. This vision is reflected in all features of the design and is carried through with high-tech and low-tech solutions, such as the use of surplus electricity to charge electric-powered bikes, a system of shared car use and the adoption of smart-card technology.

SITE PLAN

ABOVE There is a purposeful madness about BedZED, not least in the wind cowls that nod like contented beasts grazing on the green roof.

OPPOSITE The inventiveness of the scheme lies not only in its creation of a truly sustainable, well-designed community but also in the urban densities it achieves in a suburban setting of 50 homes per hectare, as well as 2500 square metres of workspace for 200 workers.

CLIENT Dickon Robinson, The Peabody Trust STRUCTURAL ENGINEER Ellis & Moore SERVICES ENGINEER Arup ENVIRONMENTAL CONSULTANT BioRegional Development CONTRACTOR Gardiner & Theobald Construction Management CONTRACT VALUE £15 million PHOTOGRAPHER ZEDfactory.com

30 FINSBURY SQUARE
.LONDON EC2
.ERIC PARRY ARCHITECTS

This is a very modern building in a highly traditional setting, and it works supremely well for its users. The concept of the building was born out of an idea for reworking the square. The most difficult part of the design was to persuade the public – through the planning process – that a new building could be as good as a locally listed building that had to be demolished; so it was essentially about conservation of the square for the future. The architects had also to contend with a design guide for the square that prefers the use of Portland stone, a vertical emphasis and a prescribed building height. A very special solution was then found to all these problems and parameters, resulting in an office environment that is stunning and a building that makes an important contribution to the square.

Unlike any speculative commercial office building completed in and around the City of London in recent years, 30 Finsbury Square owes its external appearance and its internal characteristics to the architects' bold decision to exploit the possibilities of load-bearing stone as the crucial material and structural element in the design. Dictated by the local planning authority's conservation policy, the use of stone has resulted in a deep screen on the front façade.

There is nothing arbitrary about the final result, which gives significant column-free space for the office interiors. The internal atrium is as dramatic as it is unexpected; light enters the interiors, not least the basement space, in a variety of ways. The nature of the façade changes as the eye turns the corner from the front to the rear elevations. The shift indicates an economy of thinking (as well as economy of construction) that informs this project and has offered a new proposition about the use of traditional materials in a market dominated by steel, glass and aluminium.

Offices make up 80 per cent of the fabric of the City of London, yet they have always been built pragmatically, quickly and as cheaply as possible. Façades have tended to be treated like bathroom tiling. The brilliance of this scheme is to invert such thinking by creating that load-bearing façade and by separating it from the glazed interior.

The project represents a marriage between the urban archetype of the London square and the office building, a hybrid that has produced a novel technical solution. These ground-breaking offices, although expressed as a stone building, have a heart of steel. A 15-metre clear span links the façade back to a frame construction around the atrium and core, helping to satisfy the needs of the money men of the City for large floorplates.

The detailing throughout is exquisite, and the fit-out, by different designers, is for once complementary. On the rear, north side, the windows are brought out to the face. Here the masonry is not load-bearing but instead takes the form of a rainscreen hung on a simple steel frame.

ABOVE What is most significant about this office block is the architects' use of stone as a load-bearing material.

OPPOSITE The result makes a major contribution to a sensitive London square as well as providing column-free and therefore highly lettable interiors.

CLIENT Jones Lang LaSalle STRUCTURAL ENGINEER Whitbybird CONTRACTOR HBG Construction CONTRACT VALUE £26 million PHOTOGRAPHER Hélène Binet

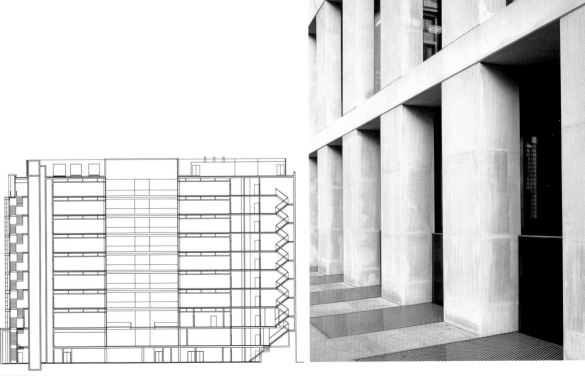

SECTION

THE GREAT COURT AT THE BRITISH MUSEUM .LONDON WC1 .FOSTER AND PARTNERS

At a stroke, the Great Court makes sense of a rambling mess of a museum that had grown haphazardly, with a bit of infill here, a supposedly temporary lean-to there, all besmirching Smirke and his magnificent Reading Room. The removal of the library to the Euston Road has liberated the full potential of the British Museum at last. In fact, it is difficult to think of another British public building that has been so completely transformed in terms of perception and use through the introduction of such a grand yet simple concept.

The strength of the project lies in the clarity of this central idea: turning the building outside in, converting a forgotten courtyard into the primary space, thus creating a public focus and linking galleries previously only accessible in a linear, prescribed route. The Great Court enables a different experience of galleries, vertically and horizontally, allowing visitors to enjoy their own selection of exhibits, free from the usual chronological sequence. Smirke's Reading Room, previously hidden and inaccessible, is now placed at the heart of the museum, visible from various levels and from outside as well as in.

While the glazed roof and central stone addition to the Reading Room are the most obvious parts of the project, much of the £100 million scheme involves reworking the depths of the museum to provide excellent lecture and education spaces, again easily accessed from the public concourse and enriching the experience of the museum. The quality of the design and construction, however, also lies in the detail, which creates a consistent, controlled language that engages with the original building.

The architects specified a canopy of inflated ETFE pillows on the grounds of their thermal characteristics and capacity to block ultraviolet radiation. The roof sections were prefabricated off site and lowered into position with the use of lasers. When the roof was depropped, the structure dropped 150 millimetres and spread 90 millimetres, like a sheet of silk. It behaved exactly as predicted by the engineers: complex geometry translated into reality.

The impression on walking through the new portico is dramatic, amplified by the gloom of the previous spaces. The shadow play from the roof structure on a sunny day adds greatly to the character of the space. Two sweeping staircases flanking the Reading Room greet those approaching through the main entrance, and their inviting appearance successfully draws visitors to the temporary exhibition gallery and the restaurant on the upper levels, while also permitting powerful elevated views down into the court. The Great Court is a welcome and powerful addition to the rich cultural experiences of London and a very good example of a design team all working together to produce a marriage of architecture and engineering.

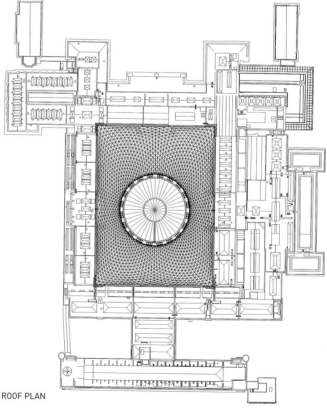

ROOF PLAN

CLIENT The British Museum HISTORIC BUILDING ADVISORS Giles Quarme & Associates/Caroe & Partners/Ian Bristow STRUCTURAL AND M&E ENGINEER Buro Happold CONTRACTOR Mace CONTRACT VALUE £100 million PHOTOGRAPHER Nigel Young – Foster and Partners

TOP AND OPPOSITE, TOP AND BOTTOM LEFT Seldom has a scheme so successfully liberated a building from its nineteenth- and twentieth-century convolutions. Norman Foster's Great Court has made a new covered square out of gash space no one knew existed.

OPPOSITE, BOTTOM RIGHT Seen from the tower of the University of London's Senate House, the pin-cushion roof is even more magical than when viewed from below.

and let thy feet
milenniums hence
be set in midst of knowledge

PLYMOUTH THEATRE ROYAL PRODUCTION CENTRE
.PLYMOUTH, DEVON .IAN RITCHIE ARCHITECTS

Ian Ritchie is an artist and a poet as well as an architect. Here, on a scruffy bit of coast beyond the last of Plymouth's terraces, there is a scraggy area of tin sheds and culs-de-sac. On the edge of a small harbour, amid the grimy glamour of a half-derelict industrial zone, Ritchie has found inspiration for the kind of work he does best – an arts building for a highly imaginative client. But this is more workaday than your average arts building; this is a backstage building for the Theatre Royal in a backstage place.

Ritchie clearly relished the brief and the location. He has made a robust factory-like building on the edge of the water. The ground is reclaimed from the harbour and forms a raised storm barrier. It is made from broken stone and it slopes in a long, even line down to the sea. The building is placed with artistic care on this pulverized rock podium.

The building is organized into three clear parts: a long bar of workshops relating to the manufacture of stage sets, a large shed for their assembly, and a series of independent rooms for rehearsal. The three elements are clearly articulated, and different cladding materials signify each one. The workshops are wrapped in a standing-seam zinc, the shed is clad in an almost matching opalescent glass to allow even illumination of the interior, and the rehearsal rooms are kitted out in a fabulous quilted anorak of phosphor-bronze mesh.

The interior of the building, by contrast, is very matter of fact. Simple materials and clear graphics signify the working nature of the place. The industrial elements are set as a simple, functional nave, with set assembly, workshops, dressing, costume, offices and restrooms linked along a 'straight as a die' glazed route stretching from reception to service entrance. The Crittall windows to the rehearsal spaces afford often surprising views of passing shipping. The main construction workshop is double-height, allowing sufficient headroom for complete sets to be constructed and assembled. So rare is this facility that the theatre undertakes work for outside companies, including the Royal Opera, thus helping the new centre to pay for itself.

The rehearsal rooms sit on the rock armour platform as if they were objects of contemplation. They are like nothing else – half coat of chain mail, half puffa-jacket. Lifted off the ground by a tilted ring of glass, they are made to float. This is pure architectural drama. Ritchie plays with our perception of weight, mass and materials.

It is fortunate that the client found the right architect for this programme and place. Ritchie's muted, almost bitter, palate has conjured a strange, awkward beauty from this barren stretch of shore.

LEFT Internally, these are practical working spaces, cheaply built and robust.

OPPOSITE The poetry is saved for the outside, where the bronze-mesh-covered structures are scattered on a rocky beach as if by a receding tide.

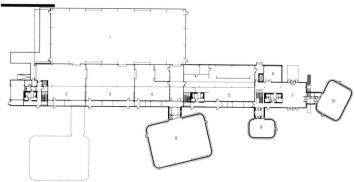

GROUND-FLOOR PLAN

CLIENT Plymouth Theatre Royal STRUCTURAL AND M&E ENGINEER Arup
CONTRACTOR Bluestone CONTRACT VALUE £5.8 million PHOTOGRAPHER Ian Ritchie

TIREE SHELTER – AN TURAS
.TIREE, INNER HEBRIDES .SUTHERLAND HUSSEY ARCHITECTS

An Turas is Gaelic for journey; here the journey, albeit a short one, involves all the senses. As you enter the narrow tunnel, the wind is deadened; human voices are heightened but change as you walk its length between the hard white walls (almost blinding in sudden sunshine) that cut through a sloping hillside, through the timber-slatted covered bridge across a rocky outcrop, finally to emerge into the glass and steel belvedere that crashes through a traditional dry-stone wall and frames a view of a white dot of a building on the far shore. This is architecture and art made inseparable.

This is a place of peace, in contrast to the chaos of impressions that greet the visitor at the nearby pierhead. Although tiny, the collaborative project between two architects, four artists and an engineer reflects many of the monumental qualities of the place: the big sky and horizon, the white beach, the monochromatic black houses dotted over the land, all distilled as a line in the landscape. It is both artwork and viewing platform. Looking down the passageway from the shelter's entrance, you see a framed view across the bay of a perfectly ordinary stretch of flat, treeless, brightly lit Tiree. But as you approach and arrive at the glass box, the picture opens up and is made magical. Essentially this is a telescope that, once

entered, frames an exquisite fragment of sky, house, foreshore, beach and water. In a landscape where all is battened down to survive the gales, the pavilion elevates the soul, providing an appropriately calm oasis amid the ugliness of contemporary life.

A very moving piece of architectural sculpture has been created out of the mundane requirement for a tiny shelter from the wind. This is both the sunniest and the windiest place in the United Kingdom. So although it is a low-level linear structure, strength was essential. And because the rendered walls are unroofed, they need to be self-supporting to withstand regular 110-kph winds. The glass box had to be made up on the mainland and was transported and craned into position – an expensive and even hazardous procedure necessitated by a lack of skilled labour on the island.

The shelter is not treated reverentially, either by people or by its surroundings. One islander said, yes, it frames the view, but the view was fine without it; others refer to it as two walls and a telephone box with no phone. Yet the islanders have come to respect, even love it, and are excited by the attention it and their island have received. In many ways, the shelter sums up their island: a low and white building, crouched against the wind, a thing of mystery and strange beauty.

LEFT AND BELOW Certainly the cheapest, probably the oddest structure yet to make it on to the Stirling shortlist, the Tiree Shelter delights visitors by being "beyond function".

OPPOSITE In plan and section, Sutherland Hussey's designs perfectly reflect what is to be seen on the ground: an object that reflects and enhances the tough landscape in which it sits.

CLIENT Tiree Arts Enterprise **ARTISTS** Jake Harvey/Sandra Kennedy/ Glen Onwin/Donald Urquhart **STRUCTURAL ENGINEER** David Narro Associates **CONTRACTOR** Inscape Joinery **CONTRACT VALUE** £95,000 **PHOTOGRAPHER** Donald Urquhart

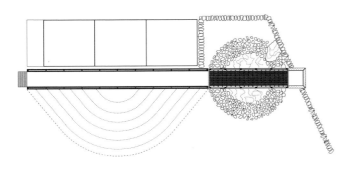

PLAN AND SECTION

THE STIRLING PRIZE 2003
.KENNETH POWELL
ARCHITECTURE CRITIC, JOURNALIST AND WRITER

The Stirling Prize has been hugely significant in generating increased public interest in architecture. For architects and critics, however, the race for the Stirling starts even before the Awards Group publishes the longlist (as it were) of projects in Britain and abroad that have secured RIBA Awards.

It was obvious from day one that Herzog & de Meuron's Laban would be a strong contender for the Stirling in 2003. Tate Modern had put the already highly rated Swiss practice on the world map. (It had missed out on the RIBA Awards because Herzog & de Meuron was not yet eligible.) But Tate was a conversion; Laban was a new building, visually striking and with the added advantage of being a component in the regeneration strategy for Deptford. There was plenty of potential competition. Foster and Partners' Great Court at the British Museum and Millennium Bridge in London were both potential winners. There was the excellent National Maritime Museum Cornwall at Falmouth by Long & Kentish, the English Heritage Visitor Centre at Whitby Abbey in Yorkshire by Stanton Williams, and the Baltic centre for contemporary art in Gateshead, a transformation by Ellis Williams of a redundant flour mill that was certainly very much about regeneration. (The adjacent Millennium Bridge by Wilkinson Eyre had won the Stirling in 2002.) The Centre for Mathematical Sciences at Cambridge by Edward Cullinan Architects showed this long-established and much respected practice in excellent form. Cultural and educational buildings in this mould are always well placed to win the accolade.

When the list of RIBA Awards emerged, there were other jewels to discover: schools by Allford Hall Monaghan Morris and Penoyre & Prasad; a laboratory building in Germany by Sauerbruch Hutton Architects; no fewer than eight winners in Manchester; and some exceptional houses, some by famous names (Chipperfield, Fretton), others by newer talents (Azman Owens, Tonkin Liu, Jamie Fobert). A private house has yet, however, to win the Stirling, although Fobert's Anderson House won the 2003 Manser Medal, one of the special awards. Another sparkling project by a young firm, Centaur Street housing by De Rijke Marsh Morgan, took the *AJ* First Building Award. Philip Gumuchdjian, shortlisted for that award, walked off with the Stephen Lawrence Prize for an exquisite riverside retreat in Ireland.

A comparable exercise in *jeu d'esprit*, Sutherland Hussey's An Turas shelter in remote Tiree ended up on the Stirling shortlist. Described by one of the judges as "a spiritual experience ... beyond function", it attracted a lot of public votes and could have been a winner. Channel 4's coverage of the Stirling has undoubtedly transformed the prize. Buildings with an agenda, a clear narrative, have an appeal that extends beyond the assessment of purely architectural quality. Bill Dunster Architects' BedZED housing in Wallington, Surrey, another hotly tipped contender, certainly had an agenda, that of sustainability. Dunster's ambition to create Britain's first 'carbon-neutral' housing scheme had won the support of an inspirational client, the Peabody Trust. Aware of the project's environmental credentials, some of the judges went there expecting "hair-shirt worthiness". They were agreeably surprised by the exuberance of the architecture, although some found the treatment of the external spaces – some private gardens accessible only by bridges – eccentric. The project demanded attention and analysis, although Dunster has subsequently had difficulty securing clients and sites for further developments.

Office blocks, like private houses, are not obvious Stirling winners. Maybe there are memories of the days (not so many years ago) when good architects did not soil their hands with commercial commissions. Yet the design of the workplace – and today most people work in offices – is as demanding and significant a challenge as that of mass housing. Richard Rogers Partnership's environmentally progressive office buildings at Chiswick Park and its streetwise, precisely detailed Broadwick Street offices won awards in 2003, as did office projects by Reiach and Hall, Architecture PLB, Allford Hall Monaghan Morris and Kohn Pedersen Fox. But it was Eric Parry's 30 Finsbury Square that ended up on the Stirling shortlist, not for its internal spaces (relatively conventional) but for its public face. Parry's finely crafted, load-bearing façade of Portland stone could be seen as a generous, civic-minded, if sober, gesture on the part of the developer.

Ian Ritchie's Production Centre for the Theatre Royal in Plymouth, in contrast, lacked a civic dimension. Sited in a dead-end industrial backwater by the River Plym, it had to be sought out. It was "a backstage building in a backstage place". Ritchie is one of the stars of his generation in what used to be called the 'high-tech' tradition. His practice has built rather less in this country than one might expect. A Ritchie building is always a cause for celebration. His intuitive use of materials was shown to good effect in the Plymouth project, which seems to take its cue from the local shipbuilding tradition. To describe the aesthetic of the building, containing workshops, stores and rehearsal spaces, as 'industrial', however, would be to ignore the subdued richness of its cladding, in particular the phosphor-bronze mesh that wraps the rehearsal rooms. This is an outstanding building that could hardly have failed to make the shortlist. The same could be said of Norman Foster's Great Court (completed, in fact, in 2000). The project transformed the visitor's experience of the British Museum, equipping the place to deal with the huge numbers it attracts, and gave London a spectacular covered public space, claimed to be the largest in Europe. With the redesign of the front quadrangle and the creation of new galleries for the ethnographic collections, the scheme gave Britain a project to rival Paris's Grand Louvre. Foster, winner of the Stirling in 1998, was to win the prize again in 2004 for the iconic Swiss Re tower, 30 St Mary Axe, proving that commercial buildings can be winners.

In the end, however, the Stirling Prize for 2003 rightly went to Laban. The project had a fascinating history and an inspirational client in Dr Marion North. It was a remarkable integration of architecture and art, with Michael Craig-Martin working in close harmony with the architects. The internal landscape of the building was revelatory and hugely enjoyable (although students subsequently complained of the "goldfish bowl" nature of the studios). The external landscape, not in place when the Stirling jury visited, has given the project a further dimension in the context of Deptford Creek. How sad that other new developments in the area were of such banal quality. Had I been on the jury, Laban would have been my choice. But where are the successor projects in this country by Herzog & de Meuron?

2004

.JUDGES

Ted Cullinan Architect [chair]

Isabel Allen Editor of *The Architects' Journal*

Deborah Bull Dancer

Antony Gormley Sculptor

Francine Houben Architect

.THE STIRLING PRIZE WINNER

.THE STIRLING PRIZE SHORTLIST

.THE STIRLING PRIZE 2004

30 ST MARY AXE
.LONDON EC3
.FOSTER AND PARTNERS

The client, Swiss Re, wanted a landmark building and it has certainly got it from Foster and Partners. It has not just got a shiny new logo for its previously little-known reinsurance business; it also has a building that is loved by Londoners, a forty-storey tapering tower that is a popular icon on the city skyline.

The first office building to win the RIBA Stirling Prize, 30 St Mary Axe is also the first building to be voted for unanimously by the Stirling judges, who were keen to stress the key role played by Swiss Re's Sara Fox.

The architects describe 30 St Mary Axe as "the capital's first environmentally progressive tall building". And indeed it takes many of the ideas about naturally ventilated high-rises – such as drawing fresh air through the light wells that spiral up the building – from the same practice's Commerzbank in Frankfurt. The winding-round of these spaces is played against two other moves: first, the tapering of the tower (the obvious factor in its being dubbed the 'Gherkin'), and second, the decision to offer lessees the choice of 'six-pack' or 'two-pack' options – in other words, units of six floors or two floors. The light wells are triangular on plan, and six of them divide the otherwise continuous ring of offices on each floor into six segments. Each of these roughly rectangular segments therefore benefits from being close to a pair of spiralling voids (whether of two or six storeys). This system is modified at the upper floors, where the building's geometry starts to squeeze in, creating some interesting spaces.

What this complex three-dimensional geometry achieves for the building is not only clever but also intelligent. The light wells, in addition to breaking up the office areas into well-proportioned chunks and providing atria and spatial interest, primarily serve to bring light and air right into the depth of the building. The office areas work equally well whether open-plan or subdivided with glass walls. The only slight disappointment is that the client has turned away from the Foster concept of hanging gardens, which in Frankfurt so successfully add to the building's oxygen supply.

One side of the office zone adjacent to a light well is offered as a communal service area. Usually – and particularly in high-rise developments – such areas are relegated to some windowless corner. Here, by contrast, whether socializing, photocopying or making tea, staff can benefit from magnificent views of the City of London at their feet.

The architects have made the most of the benefits of the tapering volume at pedestrian level too. Unlike in the earlier versions of this scheme, where the building took up the whole site, the reduction in the building's girth at ground level allows for through routes, helping knit the City back together. Also, the

PAGES 184–85 Of all the gin joints in all the towns in all the world, Norman Foster's bar has much the best views.

ABOVE AND OPPOSITE The Gherkin's characteristic shape may well be key to the building's environmental strategy, but it is equally about adding a talking point to the London skyline.

CLIENT Swiss Re STRUCTURAL ENGINEER Arup MAIN CONTRACTOR Skanska Construction UK CONTRACT VALUE Confidential PHOTOGRAPHER Grant Smith

relatively small footprint of a circular building frees up additional precious ground space for landscaping. Low walls and seats marking the historic boundaries of the site (formerly the site of the Baltic Exchange) define a public plaza giving safe access to the double-height shops at ground-floor level. The aerodynamic form also means that there are fewer downdraughts than with a rectilinear building. Another effect of the tapering form is that from close-up it is impossible to take in the whole of the building, so that the bulk one would usually associate with a 46,000-square-metre structure is greatly reduced.

Internally, the ground-floor lift lobby is suitably elegant, and the bar area at the top responds to the challenge and opportunity of elevation, situation and 360-degree views, making it one of the very best rooms in twenty-first-century London. At last London is getting back the vantage points it deserves. If only security limitations allowed the tower to be publicly accessible.

The sophistication in the handling of a clever idea that provides atmospheric space rather than just office space, the careful detailing and, at the same time, the sheer power of the structure combine to sustain the initial impression that this is a memorable building that contributes not only to the skyline of London but also to the world stage of high-rise building.

After winning the award, client Sara Fox turned letting agent, with some success. One of tenants for the ground-floor retail space – which is helping give life to the square – is a restaurant called Sterling, a neat if mis-spelled tribute to the prize.

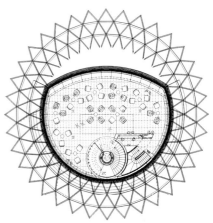

LEVEL 40 FLOOR PLAN

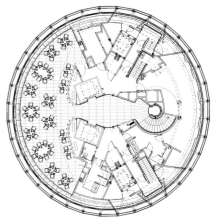

LEVEL 39 FLOOR PLAN

THE BUSINESS ACADEMY BEXLEY
.ERITH, KENT
.FOSTER AND PARTNERS

The Business Academy in Thamesmead is a ruthlessly simple steel-framed glass box with the east and west façades protected by moveable vertical aluminium louvres that shut down automatically at dusk, rendering the building vandalproof. Inside, this is about as open-plan as a school can get, with classrooms opening on to two atria. Even the classrooms with walls, such as the science laboratories, are predominantly glazed. Apart from the sophisticated external louvres, the environmental control systems are simple, and the overall efficiency of building form makes this a low-energy structure.

A business academy doesn't sound like much fun, but this one is. It's a very special and very different school that would not look out of place in a business park. The risky strategy of offering young students such a traditionally adult building form seems to have paid off. Apparently, the same group of students who had trashed their previous classroom arrived at this new school voluntarily wearing suits. Of course, there was a touch of irony about it, but since then they've come to thrive on the respect the building pays them. Foster and Partners has turned its facility with offices to the world of education and come up with a school where results are proving that good architecture makes people's lives better.

The Business Academy Bexley does what ground-breaking architecture ought to do: it makes you rethink the function of the building it houses. Here the educational thinking and the architectural thinking go hand in hand. The organization is legible and deceptively simple, incorporating spaces that are usually given special architectural treatment (for example, the theatre) undemonstratively into the whole.

The Business Academy appears to be a bold first step in transforming its desolate surroundings and restoring pride to the local community. When the judges visited, the old school, boarded-up and covered with graffiti, sat moodily next door awaiting demolition, a part of the Thamesmead experiment soon to be erased. Beside it, the future of education is shiny, even a little corporate, but also humane, and this is reflected in the vast collage in the main entrance atrium that comprises individual portrait photographs of every student.

It feels as if the academy cost more to build than most schools, and it did, though not dramatically more. But at the same time it is cheaper to run in both energy and maintenance terms. And because there are almost no secret places, there is also no vandalism to repair and no graffiti to remove, and there is far less bullying. So perhaps one of the lessons this building teaches us is that school buildings should not be too cheap. This is a building that demonstrates respect for its population of underprivileged pupils and for its staff, and receives their respect in return. It is a building that should touch each of their lives.

ABOVE The architects have created a vandalproof box, appropriate to its tough setting.

OPPOSITE This is all about the interior, where the pupils are treated very much as adults with an atrium design worthy of the most corporate of corporate headquarters.

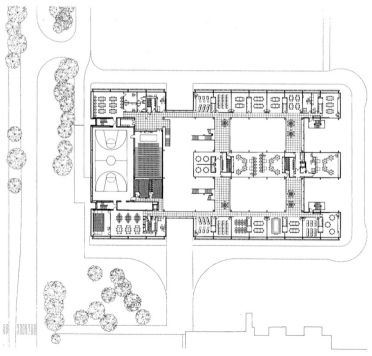

GROUND-FLOOR PLAN

CLIENT Garrard Education Trust **SPONSORS** Sir David and Lady Garrard **STRUCTURAL ENGINEER** Buro Happold **CONTRACTOR** Exterior International **CONTRACT VALUE** Confidential **PHOTOGRAPHER** Nigel Young – Foster and Partners

IMPERIAL WAR MUSEUM NORTH
.MANCHESTER
.STUDIO DANIEL LIBESKIND

The Imperial War Museum North, on the banks of the Manchester Ship Canal, takes the form of the shards of a shattered globe. The skewed Air Shard Tower marks the entrance to an extraordinary exhibition that honours the dead of twentieth-century conflicts without ever glorifying war. Three audio-visual shows transfix audiences with images of war and the voices of its participants and victims. This is architectural theatre at its very best.

The museum was built to house some of the London parent museum's unseen collections and bring them to new audiences in the North, but it does far more than that. As the client, Jim Forrester, points out, the commission presented a triple challenge: to overcome contemporary distaste for things imperial, for anything to do with war, and for museums themselves. Daniel Libeskind has risen brilliantly to the challenge with his physical commentary on the pity of war. His highlighting of the poetry of the three shards almost blinds us to the museum's practicalities, such as the clever way in which the main floor is raised up to the first floor to minimize the impact on the contaminated site and to provide vast external (and therefore low-cost) plant rooms in the undercroft.

There is no doubt that the building disorientates the visitor, as it was intended to do; even the entrance is not where one expects, facing the footbridge leading from the Lowry art gallery, but on the Trafford side. Once through the door, visitors are in an inside-outside space, the Air Shard Tower, which is clad in extruded box-section planks. In the main hall the objects sit on the gently and irregularly raking floor among the fractured rhomboids that contain within them separate exhibitions linked by a timeline; the rhomboids' external walls provide projection surfaces for 'the big show', with sixty projectors.

The £20 million project was originally a £30 million one. The budget cut meant that not only was one whole shard lost, but the cladding was changed from concrete to steel, a change for the better. It is one of the most impressive features of the project that within this reduced budget Libeskind has managed to maintain an intensity and integrity of detail and a sparse but carefully controlled palette of materials. This creative ingenuity extends to all the spaces of the building, from the drama of the galleries to the turntable display cabinets in the shop, and even to the offices with their complementary storage and furniture. The building can be enjoyed at the most accessible level of its formal resolutions and contrasts, such as the vertiginous ascent of the tower and the cave-like exhibition settings, but it also allows for a number of readings and metaphorical associations.

Le Corbusier once argued for an end to symbolism in buildings; here Libeskind has made another powerful case for the argument that buildings can have meaning beyond function.

CLIENT Trustees Imperial War Museum North ASSOCIATE ARCHITECT Leach Rhodes Walker STRUCTURAL ENGINEER Arup EXHIBITION DESIGN Real Studios CONTRACTOR Sir Robert McAlpine CONTRACT VALUE £19.7 million PHOTOGRAPHER Len Grant

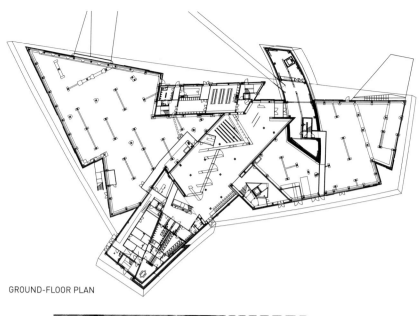

GROUND-FLOOR PLAN

ABOVE Daniel Libeskind's interiors are, as ever, intended to disconcert, whether in the Air Shard Tower (centre) or in the main exhibition space (seen above during an audio-visual show).

OPPOSITE Libeskind's shards amply demonstrate that buildings can have meaning beyond function.

KUNSTHAUS
.GRAZ, AUSTRIA .PETER COOK AND COLIN FOURNIER

Known as the 'Friendly Alien', this Austrian cultural centre is a multiskinned building, with the outer layer being made of eye-catching curved blue acrylic panels, and the inner one comprising a metal frame over which is stretched a fine metallic mesh. Two concrete decks house the museum spaces, which are linked by travelators. At night the curved façade is animated by a matrix of a thousand pulsing lights that spell out messages or display digital art.

This is the architects' first building, but when you realize that one of them is in his sixties and has already won one of architecture's top prizes, the Royal Gold Medal, for his teaching and theory, then the quality of this blue amoeba with its roof covered in suckers is less surprising. Peter Cook was the leading light of Archigram, the group that inspired generations of architects with its wacky ideas about buildings and cities. With fellow teacher Colin Fournier, he has finally realized some of those theories forty years on.

For a building to be adopted as a symbol of a city so quickly and also to be loved suggests something special is going on. But the Kunsthaus is much more than a static object for aesthetic contemplation. It is a building that demands to be experienced and, crucially, moved through and around. The effect is visceral, sometimes shocking, but ultimately joyful.

A video by Viennese film-makers Coop 99 shows the 'Friendly Alien' hovering over the city before nestling down in its new setting. The Kunsthaus is surprisingly gentle to Graz and its inhabitants, yet people stand and stare, always with smiles on their faces.

Inside, the building is designed as a journey. There is no pompous institutional threshold here, but a real openness and welcome, with reception area, lecture space and café spilling into one another. A sloping travelator imparts a sense of drama and anticipation to the entering of the galleries. Another travelator takes visitors up to the top gallery, from which they take the stairs up to the final level, the so-called 'Needle', a long glazed space projecting precariously over the roof-tops, which provides a welcome release back to the city after the intensity of the galleries.

This is not architecture that should be judged against normal values of refinement or aesthetics; in a way its very bagginess is its most appealing and humane feature. The Kunsthaus transcends limits in providing a new architectural experience that welcomes engagement, enjoyment and exhilaration. This is architecture for fun, and why not?

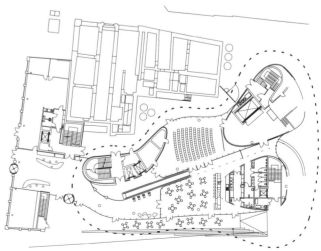

LEVEL 0 PLAN

CLIENT Kunsthaus LOCAL ARCHITECT Architektur Consult STRUCTURAL ENGINEER Bollinger und Grohmann LIGHTING DESIGN Kress & Adams CONTRACTOR SFL CONTRACT VALUE €40 million PHOTOGRAPHER Colin Fournier

OPPOSITE The Kunsthaus is designed as a journey. Travelators link the floors and add to the sense of anticipation in the visitor.

ABOVE AND RIGHT Is it a blue whale? Is it an elevated tram stop? No, it's Archigram arriving spectacularly, if forty years late, in Graz.

PHOENIX INITIATIVE
.COVENTRY, WEST MIDLANDS .MacCORMAC JAMIESON PRICHARD

The *cause célèbre* of post-war city planning in the aftermath of the Blitz that destroyed its medieval cathedral, and a paradigm in the field of traffic segregation and pedestrianization, Coventry had fallen from grace in the last quarter of the twentieth century and was in desperate need of some loving care and attention. It got all that and more from MacCormac Jamieson Prichard and the design team.

The scheme successfully creates quality public open spaces out of the formerly run-down Cathedral Quarter and manages to forge visible and physical connections between significant site levels. It also makes legible the various superimposed layers of Coventry's religious history, and yet directly addresses the difficult urban issue of how to live in a retail-orientated post-industrial culture. Perhaps the single most impressive aspect of this thoughtful scheme is that it does not rely on one key historical element or new intervention. The complex and sometimes conflicting requirements of the brief are revealed and integrated within an accessible and well-constructed civic environment of stone, steel, glass and water. The highlights include Millennium Place, with Françoise Schein's Time Zone Clock; Alex Beleschenko's blue glass bridge and Susanna Heron's dramatic water feature in Priory Place; a visitors' interpretation centre; a mixed-use development comprising eighty-four apartments and 300 square metres of retail; accommodation for cathedral staff;

and a new entrance for the Coventry Transport Museum. All these are held together in a sequence that is broadly chronological, moving down the hill from the medieval remains of the original priory to the modernity of Millennium Place. This piazza is framed by the Whittle Arch, commemorating the local inventor of the jet engine. This is not an artwork, but appropriately architecture and engineering in equal part, and is the result of a sketch doodled by MacCormac during a frustrating meeting with the planners.

At a time when so much urban regeneration is focused on the production of individual buildings, it is rare to come across a scheme that is as much about the spaces between buildings as it is about the buildings themselves.

The collaboration involves more than a risk-taking client and a sensitive architect; it also involves a large number of artists and engineers. The considered integration of art, landscape and architecture, together with issues that are so often afterthoughts (for example, traffic engineering), provides a coherence that is a model for other local authorities to follow. In one move, a bold city council has used architecture and urban design not only to make better places, but also to put itself on the European map. It has taken cities such as Barcelona and Manchester to show that publicly led regeneration really does work; now the people of Coventry have something to be proud of once again. The initiative has given them new heart and their city a new heart too.

CLIENT Coventry City Council EXECUTIVE ARCHITECT [PHASE II] PCPT Architects LANDSCAPE ARCHITECT Rumney Design Associates ART CONSULTANT Vivien Lovell – Modus Operandi Art Consultants ARTISTS Alex Beleschenko/Chris Browne/ Jochen Gerz/Susanna Heron/David Morley/Françoise Schein/David Ward/ Kate Whiteford STRUCTURAL ENGINEERS Babtie (Harris & Sutherland)/Dewhurst Macfarlane/Whitbybird CONTRACTORS Balfour Beatty/Butterley Construction/ Galliford Try CONTRACT VALUE £50 million PHOTOGRAPHER Mark Goodwin

ABOVE The Phoenix Initiative has a natural rhythm to it as it moves down the hill from the cathedral, with places to pass through (Priory Place, left) and places to rest (Garden of International Friendship, right).

OPPOSITE Millennium Place, with its Time Zone Clock by Françoise Schein and the refaced Coventry Transport Museum, is framed by Alex Beleschenko's blue glass bridge and Richard MacCormac's Whittle Arch.

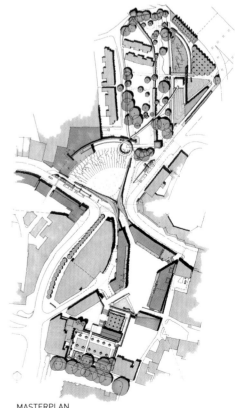

MASTERPLAN

THE SPIRE
.DUBLIN, IRELAND
.IAN RITCHIE ARCHITECTS

Remarkably, the Spire is one of three shortlisted projects in 2004 that rose from the wreckage of bombings (30 St Mary Axe is on the site of the Baltic Exchange, bombed by the IRA; and Coventry was flattened by the German air force during World War II).

Dubliners were unsurprisingly sceptical when an Englishman won the competition to replace that imperial symbol, Nelson's Pillar, which had been blown up by the IRA in the 1960s. But most people today, even the taxi drivers, have been won over by the simple beauty of Ian Ritchie's 120-metre-high stainless steel spire. They like the fact that it's more a celebration of the future than it is a memorial to the past.

In the 1960s Dublin was struggling economically, but by the 1990s, when the competition was held to replace the column, it was a different place. Ireland was undergoing the greatest economic boom in its history. The whole city was being regenerated. Ireland's outlook, linked to both the United States and the European Union, had changed beyond recognition.

It would be easy to assume that the design of a 120-metre-high single object in an open urban context would be a simple matter. Nothing could be further from the truth. Every single decision, from the diameter of the base to the materials used, the landscape context and the lighting regime, required intense thought on the part of both the architect and the associated consultants. The result is a true icon for a European capital city confident of itself and its ability to produce cultural statements of significance.

The Spire is first visible across the Dublin skyline as an object of extreme delicacy, the scale of which it is impossible to guess. Once you know what you are looking at, the anticipation of seeing how the needle hits the ground begins to grow. When it is finally revealed along O'Connell Street, the slenderness of the whole is remarkable, but in this context, set within the broad and newly landscaped street, the Spire takes on the identity of a civic monument – significant but not necessarily dominating its context.

If the Spire is approached on the east–west axis, the effect is different again. Here the relatively narrow width and small scale of Henry and Talbot streets, with their tight bustle of people, closely frame the Spire, and it becomes a city landmark, terminating the vista and constantly changing in response to light and sky. To watch the constant flow of people brushing past the base of the Spire suggests that this technically (and politically) challenging project has swiftly been adopted by Dublin as a natural part of the city fabric.

This is also 'day-for-night' architecture, in which the more celebratory side to this urban marker comes into play. The apparent effortlessness of the Spire belies the long and difficult business of bringing it into being.

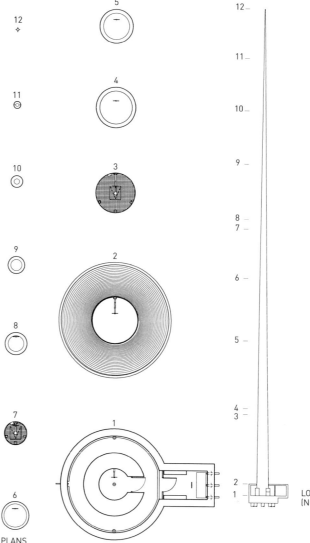

PLANS

LOCATION OF PLANS
(NOT TO SCALE)

CLIENT Dublin City Council STRUCTURAL AND M&E ENGINEER Arup CONTRACTOR SIAC Radley Joint Venture CONTRACT VALUE £3.07 million PHOTOGRAPHER Barry Mason

OPPOSITE Ian Ritchie's 120-metre-high tapering section spire has a floor area of just 7 square metres, making it the most expensive building in the world at £428,671 per square metre. Dubliners think it's worth it.

ABOVE AND RIGHT The Spire has given Dubliners a monument that celebrates the city's present and future more than it commemorates its past.

THE STIRLING PRIZE 2004
.EDWIN HEATHCOTE
ARCHITECTURE CRITIC OF THE *FINANCIAL TIMES*

The year 2004 was a pivotal one for architecture, the year of the icon. It was the year when international cities competed with each other for the most eye-catching, most publicity-generating archi-tourist attraction. The icon, an architectural type formerly limited to expos from the Crystal Palace and Eiffel Tower to the Skylon, rose to prominence in the wake of Gehry's Guggenheim in Bilbao and the realization on behalf of municipalities and depressed industrial towns everywhere that a headline piece of architecture by one of the emerging band of international starchitects could generate and attract not only PR but also tourism, low-cost airlines, finance, property speculation and international profile. That Bilbao had undergone a radical and intelligent series of urban interventions that laid the infrastructure for later success was somehow elbowed into the background. If only we too could have an icon, wailed the mayors.

Dublin got Ian Ritchie's extremely elegant, very spiky and attenuated needle, a remarkable memorial that manages to symbolize nothing, a positive achievement in a city where everything is given poetic meaning, where everything is read iconographically. Gritty Manchester, *en route* from post-industrial dereliction to loft-living urbanity, had its world shattered. Or at least got a broken globe courtesy of the king of tragedy. In the Imperial War Museum North, Daniel Libeskind created the tragic riposte to the ecstatic repose of Jørn Utzon's Sydney Opera House, the world's modern architectural ur-icon. A sphere on its way back from the breaker's yard, perhaps just along the Ship Canal, it sits easily but theatrically in its setting. Perhaps the ultimate cipher for iconism, the structure constitutes an unsatisfactory museum bred with an undeniably powerful image, a building in which the statement is everything. It was also an extremely important step towards making Libeskind the default architect of memorialization after his astounding Jewish Museum in Berlin and, undoubtedly, it played a role in his gaining the commission for the all but aborted Ground Zero project, still perhaps the single most controversial project of recent times.

Little Austrian Graz got Peter Cook's and Colin Fournier's extraordinary and lively Kunsthaus, probably the apotheosis, but unfortunately not the end, of the 'Blob' school. The curvaceous, insectoid building, apparently dubbed by locals the 'Friendly Alien', actually contributes much to a city with a rich history of organic architecture and is one of the few realizations of some of those 1960s dreams that had become so influential on the High-Tech movement.

So it was wonderful to see the Kunsthaus up against Foster and Partners' 30 St Mary Axe, the 'Blob' against the 'Gherkin'. Norman Foster had been at the forefront of High Tech, but had always been able to leaven the harsh Meccano aesthetic with a sensuous curve, as he showed in the Willis Faber & Dumas headquarters thirty years earlier. The 'Gherkin', as it has become universally known, was indeed an icon, a hugely powerful symbol of the City of London, and it had a massive physical impact both on the City and on its perception from the east. But it could also be argued that, through no fault of Foster's, it has proved an extremely dangerous structure. It is a building of such quality, of such immediacy and striking architectural elegance, that skyscrapers in the City are now seen almost universally as a good thing. Yet those that it continues to inspire remain a distinctly underwhelming offer.

Foster appeared again with his Bexley Business Academy, a slick, see-through Modernist box in the midst of one of the country's most dreadful failures of Modernism, the Thamesmead that so effectively provided the setting for Stanley Kubrick's reading of *A Clockwork Orange*. Corporate and cool, lightweight and transparent, the academy presented a wonderful cipher for Blair's PFI-driven education policy.

Finally, there was a rare entry for urbanism, an entry that was itself a series of artistic and architectural icons choreographed in Coventry by MacCormac Jamieson Prichard. An ambitious attempt to grow a new heart for a city that was left devastated by the twin excesses of bombs and overzealous Modernist planning, the Phoenix Initiative has the rare distinction of attempting to attain icon status while making a serious effort to connect site and structure to urban fabric, history and local lives, employing thoughtful and properly integrated public art.

At the time it seemed no surprise that Foster won; indeed, it proved almost a relief to see commercial architecture of excellence and innovation win out over the more usual worthy public buildings and, in retrospect, the decision looks even more secure. Only rarely does an icon become a good thing, and Foster's spire has become his most visible international symbol.

30 St Mary Axe was recently declared the most admired building in the world in a poll of architects. The 2004 Stirling Prize could have no greater affirmation than that extraordinary result. Inevitably awards are drawn to the daring and the adventurous, to the eye-catching and the monumental, but the danger in this is that the serious work done by architects who attempt to engage with existing urban material, who try to weave new fabric using the threads of history, memory and material, remains unrecognized and unrewarded. Most of the buildings on this list were conceived to swell with the oxygen of publicity, already having generated pages of local and national coverage. 30 St Mary Axe and the subsequent recipient of the prize, the Scottish Parliament, were worthy, perhaps even unassailable, winners, rich in architectural and sculptural invention, and both have become integrated into their respective urban fabrics (even if the latter remains deeply unpopular with Scots). But the danger remains that, in rewarding the spectacular and the special, the everyday and the ordinary, the subtle and the sophisticated can be ignored. A reflective architectural volume packed with photos of icons may set off a Noguchi coffee table, but a city spiked with towers, shards and blobs, a hedgehog metropolis rolled through a nursery table of Plasticine, creates at best an architectural theme park. It ignores the infinitely subtle grain, the barely perceptible layers, the streets, alleys and places, the curious juxtapositions and the palimpsest city. Iconitis was diagnosed, confirmed, even enjoyed in 2004, but it may not prove incurable.

2005

.JUDGES

Jack Pringle RIBA president (chair)

Isabel Allen Editor of *The Architects' Journal*

Joan Bakewell Journalist and broadcaster

Max Fordham Environmental engineer

Piers Gough Architect

.THE STIRLING PRIZE WINNER

.THE STIRLING PRIZE SHORTLIST

.THE STIRLING PRIZE 2005

THE SCOTTISH PARLIAMENT
.EDINBURGH .EMBT/RMJM

To look down on the Scottish Parliament building from Salisbury Crags is to see realized Enric Miralles's competition-winning dream, first manifest in the handful of leaves he threw down on the table to the amazement of the judges. If the later conceit of the roofs as up-turned boats is a metaphor too far, this is the appropriate one, the organic one, for the success of the project is the way it grows out of its majestic landscape setting. The result is a remarkable architectural statement that makes an enormous impact not only on visitors to the building but also on its users, who repeatedly move through a series of extraordinary spaces and their changing effects.

That a project outlived both its original client (Donald Dewar) and its architect (Miralles) and still got built and built well, is very much down to the vision and determination of one man: chief architect at the Scottish Executive, John Gibbons. This is his building every bit as much as it is Dewar's; just as it is RMJM's every bit as much as it is EMBT's. Gibbons was the man who had to ensure that the original vision of two men, who had achieved instant sainthood on their deaths and whose work could therefore not be touched, could be realized – and afforded.

The proof of the extraordinary architectural ambition and design vision is to be seen in every aspect and detail of the finished building. It makes an organic transition between the city and the drama of the Scottish countryside surrounding it. The extremely successful landscaping makes this transition even more striking. The experience of the interiors is impressive, and some of the spaces are real gems in terms of public spaces: the crypt-like entrance hall, the committee rooms (possibly the most mature pieces of architecture in the whole dizzying complex), the monastic members' offices, and above all the chamber that imbues this fledgling parliament with a sense of the country's long history. The list of admirable achievements is a long one, and the ability of both design and construction teams to realize a building of this complexity is truly remarkable.

The building is a statement of sparkling excellence. On the Memory Wall one of the statements reads, "Say little and say it well." This building is definitely saying a lot rather than little, but it definitely says it well.

Charles Jencks wrote: "This building explores new territory for Scottish identity and for architecture. In the era of the iconic building, it creates an iconology of references to nature and the locale … . Instead of being a monumental building, as is the usual capital landmark, it nestles its way into the environment, an icon of organic resolution, of knitting together nature and culture into a complex union" (*The Scottish Parliament* [London 2005]).

The Stirling judges were almost unanimous in their praise for the building. Piers Gough was particularly short in dismissing the cost over-run question: "Miralles would probably never have

CLIENT The Scottish Parliamentary Corporate Body STRUCTURAL ENGINEER Arup
CONTRACTOR Bovis Lend Lease CONTRACT VALUE £250 million PHOTOGRAPHER Keith Hunter

got another job in penny-pinching Britain." Max Fordham agreed: "All the best buildings have generous clients; it's difficult to create really great architecture on a shoestring." Gibbons explained the £200 million over-run in still more pragmatic terms: "The £40 million original quote was a political figure – what Dewar knew he could get the politicians to agree. In fact, he'd asked me what it would cost to repaint the old High School [an earlier proposed venue for the parliament] and quadrupled the answer. But it was never realistic for a new building. What's more, the brief has changed out of all recognition: the first figure was for an 11,000-square-metre building, basically just a chamber; the MSPs' offices and so on take it to 33,000 square metres. Then there's the huge added cost of post-9/11 security."

The Scottish Parliament is a once-in-a-lifetime building, and it is refreshing that, for once with a British building, a decision has been taken to spend a lot of money well, instead of an inadequate amount badly. But this was about far more than money. Gough wanted to give the parliament the Stirling Prize for "the genius of its urbanity. ...The architectural profession has to dream ... in the end the architect has to bring poetry ... and that is the really important thing architects do ... that's what we're here for ...; we mustn't be turned into monkeys working machines to build buildings. This is a passionate industry, where the architects bring to it poetry, beauty, magnificence and that's of course what the Scottish Parliament has."

PAGES 202–203 Every detail of the interior screams quality and love, whether in the chamber (main photo), one of the committee rooms (top right) or the MSPs' foyer (bottom right).

OPPOSITE The sunshades that deck much of the exterior are of oak, not bamboo, and represent the twigs – as the roofs represent the leaves – that formed part of Enric Miralles's dramatic presentation to the competition judges.

BOTTOM Fragments of rock are embedded in the Canongate wall, a reminder that a building is only borrowed from the landscape.

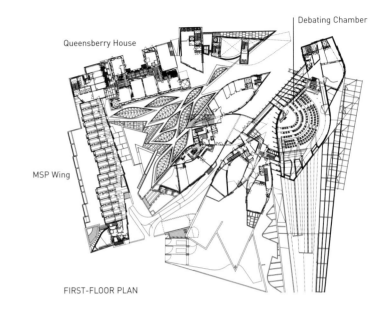

Queensberry House

Debating Chamber

MSP Wing

FIRST-FLOOR PLAN

BMW CENTRAL BUILDING AND PLANT
.LEIPZIG .GERMANY
.ZAHA HADID ARCHITECTS

The central building takes up just 26,000 of the 400,000 square metres of the whole BMW plant, which is the size of fifty football pitches. It is almost coquettish in its allure, and it is only on entering under the flying concrete bridge, into the enormous reception hall or *Marktplatz* – capable of holding 2000 people at the opening, but only a small part of what is in effect a single-volume building – that the extraordinary power of its vision is revealed.

Yes, it's immediately apparent that car production is the central function, thanks to the nice conceit of half-finished Beamers gliding along on elevated conveyor tracks, making their silent, stately way between the body shop and the paint shop, weaving above five hundred office and production staff. The embodiment of Hadid's sinuous, sensuous architecture, this is also dynamic, wholly fit for the purpose of a car plant.

Once the visitor's procession through the cavernous space begins, the organization becomes clear as the separate functions intertwine and the visitor rises through the space on gentle inclines and steps connecting a series of mezzanines. Orientation is helped by colour-coded lighting; blue, for instance, signifies maintenance. Circulation, offices and restaurants are barely delineated, and there are glimpses of cars being tested in the few fully enclosed – though only with glazing – spaces. (Instead of the 'them and us' mentality engendered by the design of most car plants, here office workers are involved in the process, and all staff are encouraged in their lunch breaks to examine the minor faults thrown up by the rigorous testing.) These are the endless variations of an evolving space. The experience is simply moving and breathtaking: powerful, serene and beautiful, all at the same time.

However, there is nothing gestural about this building. Everything is meticulously planned. It is built and detailed well, and it is clear from its commanding resolution that this radical form of a building has not just started here with this project but has been expanded and refined in Hadid's office on smaller projects, before cohering in this current building: materiality, light, space, signage, doors, door handles, WCs, balustrades, the stuff of putting it together, all flow in one seamless space.

This is a towering achievement by an architect – working again with her partner, Patrik Schumacher, and with project architect, Lars Teichmann – who has finally fulfilled her enormous and much-vaunted potential. It is hard to do justice in words to architecture of this stature. Simply, it is a monumental building that works exquisitely on all levels. This architecture has arrived.

ABOVE AND BELOW The main superstructure elements consist of precast, prestressed concrete slabs, supported on precast concrete beams and columns.

OPPOSITE There is a consistency in the quality of the concrete finishes, stairs, soffits, and, most spectacularly, the tracks on which the half-made cars glide.

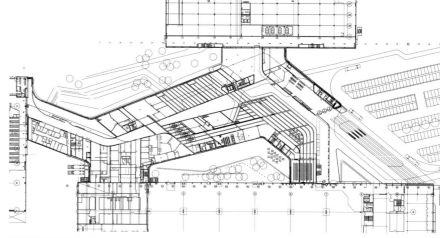

GROUND-FLOOR PLAN

CLIENT BMW Group, Munich **STRUCTURAL AND M&E ENGINEERS** AGP ARGE Gesamtplanung/Anthony Hunt Associates **CONTRACTORS** ARGE Rohbau/Wolff & Müller with OBAG **CONTRACT VALUE** €54 million **PHOTOGRAPHERS** Hélène Binet (above; opposite)/Roland Halbe (top)

FAWOOD CHILDREN'S CENTRE
.LONDON NW10 .ALSOP DESIGN

The Fawood Children's Centre was commissioned by the Stonebridge Housing Action Trust to replace an existing nursery school for three-to-five-year-olds, also to provide a small unit for children with learning disabilities (mostly autism), space for adult education, and a base for community education workers and consultation services. All this is in line with the government's Sure Start initiative for combining such facilities under one roof.

And this is quite a roof. The design concept addressed the requirements of internal and external space in an unusual yet highly commendable way, by having the accommodation as free-standing elements within a larger enclosure. The three-storey-high accommodation is made from refurbished and adapted sea containers. Under a part-translucent, part-opaque pitched roof, the enclosure is made from stainless steel mesh incorporating coloured lozenges at the upper level, where the mesh adopts a series of waved profiles. The resulting spaces between the cage and the containers accommodate different play areas and a yurt, albeit one made not in Mongolia but in Cornwall.

Will Alsop is not perhaps an architect most obviously amenable to design-and-build contracts – he was novated to the contractor, Durkan – but the shotgun marriage seems to have worked well, with time allowed for architect and subcontractor to work on mock-ups of the steel mesh. The RIBA Awards jury was particularly impressed by the concept of the 'friendly cage' enclosing functional and play areas. This device addresses the issue of how to protect children without depriving them of daylight and fresh air. Most nurseries solve the problem by placing outdoor play spaces to the rear of the building, enclosing them with far less elegant fencing than here. But the play areas are generally open to the elements and therefore of little use for large parts of the year. At Fawood the philosophy is "keep the children dry and they'll keep warm by running around". The judges also liked the way in which the cage is animated by the play of light on the coloured lozenges that stud the outer faces of the grille. And they admired the reuse of prefabricated boxes (albeit fixed and immoveable) and the fact that the accommodation is multilevel rather than single storey, adding further stimulus to the children's play. The headteacher reported that her charges seemed to be considerably healthier since the new building opened – a fine example of the beneficial effects of good architecture. She also said that some of the older siblings of the nursery attendees had commented to her that they wished they were younger again. However, there are two evenings a week of activities for older children at Fawood, with the possibility of more to come. This is a nursery but also much, much more.

Although the Stirling judges were bemused by the project when they arrived, they left having been won over by its sheer bravado, carrying away with them an impression of amusement and delight.

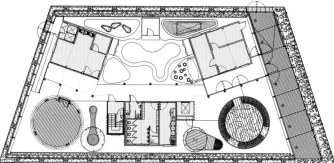

GROUND-FLOOR PLAN

ABOVE The coloured lozenges turn the stainless steel mesh from forbidding fence to friendly cage.

OPPOSITE Most nurseries place play areas at the rear, surrounded by high fences; Will Alsop's solution places them under cover but in the open air.

CLIENT Stonebridge Housing Action Trust STRUCTURAL ENGINEER Adams Kara Taylor CONTRACTOR Durkan CONTRACT VALUE £2.3 million PHOTOGRAPHER Roderick Coyne

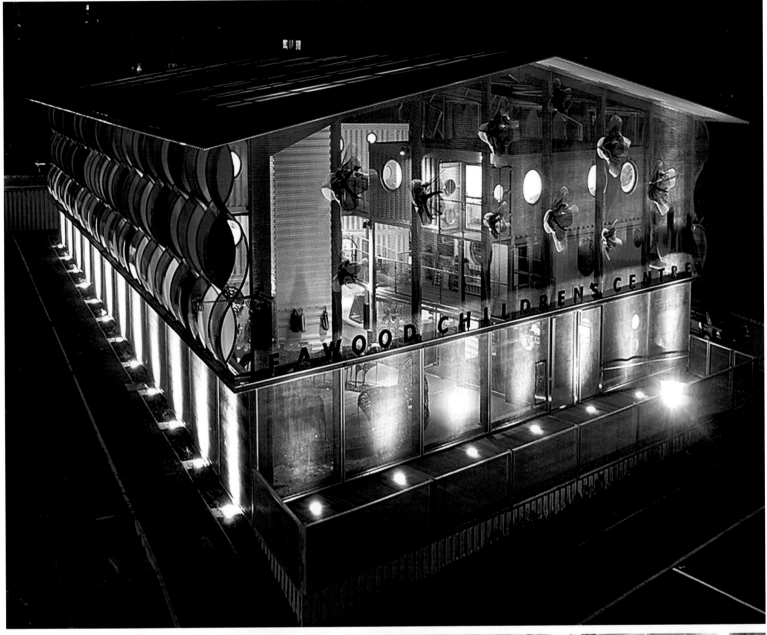

JUBILEE LIBRARY
.BRIGHTON, EAST SUSSEX .BENNETTS ASSOCIATES
WITH LOMAX CASSIDY & EDWARDS

The Jubilee Library is the centrepiece of the regeneration scheme that stitches back together the fragmented streets of the North Laine area near the centre of Brighton. This is a PFI project in which the developer cross-subsidized the building with revenue from other developments. The library strikes a direct relationship with the square of which it occupies two sides, and it is clearly intended as a civic building of importance.

The locally made blue tiles used on the façade are a reference to the use elsewhere in the city of mathematical tiles. Otherwise the library is largely glass-fronted: a simple, energy-efficient building with a good measure of style. When the rest of the square is complete with shops, hotel, offices and restaurants, a run-down quarter of Brighton will have been reinvigorated.

The main library space is excellent, with timber-clad side walls, fine concrete detailing and good natural lighting. It is both monumental and inviting. The massive white concrete columns rise to a vaulted ceiling; the effect is akin to that of being in a great Romanesque cathedral such as Durham. It is a joy to be in.

The library was designed to achieve an 'excellent' BREEAM (BRE's Environmental Assessment Method) rating for, among

other things, its low embodied energy, its low energy consumption, and its use of recycled rainwater. The building has a clear and formal plan, with the environmental engineering clearly driving the structural expression. Thick concrete was used to help achieve thermal stability, with eight free-standing concrete columns with fan-shaped heads supporting a middle floor and roof. Air is fed through voids in the concrete floorslabs supplying the perimeter rooms and the main space, with three centrally located wind towers adding to the skyline of a city known for its Regency domes.

Although this is essentially a one-volume space, different character is imparted to such areas as the children's library, the students' library and the AV collections; here the acoustic panels are so effective that it is impossible to hear the music being played until one enters the space. The library is enjoyed by both staff and users, and there is a strong public art and exhibition programme.

Two nights before the Stirling ceremony, the library won the prime minister's Better Public Building Award. Instead of being a good omen, it turned out to be a consolation prize – if winning an award the PM considers so important that he wanted to deliver it in person can be considered a runner-up prize.

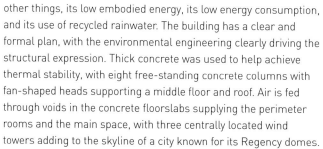

ABOVE From inside and out, Bennetts' library strikes up a relationship with the new square of which it is the focus.

OPPOSITE The quality of the internal detailing better befits a well-endowed university library than a PFI-funded public building.

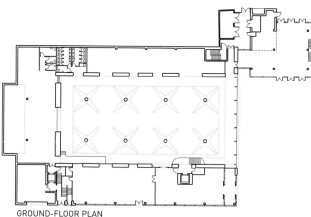
GROUND-FLOOR PLAN

CLIENT Brighton & Hove City Council **STRUCTURAL AND CIVIL ENGINEER** SKM Anthony Hunts **CONTRACTOR** Rok **CONTRACT VALUE** £8 million **PHOTOGRAPHER** Peter Cook – VIEW

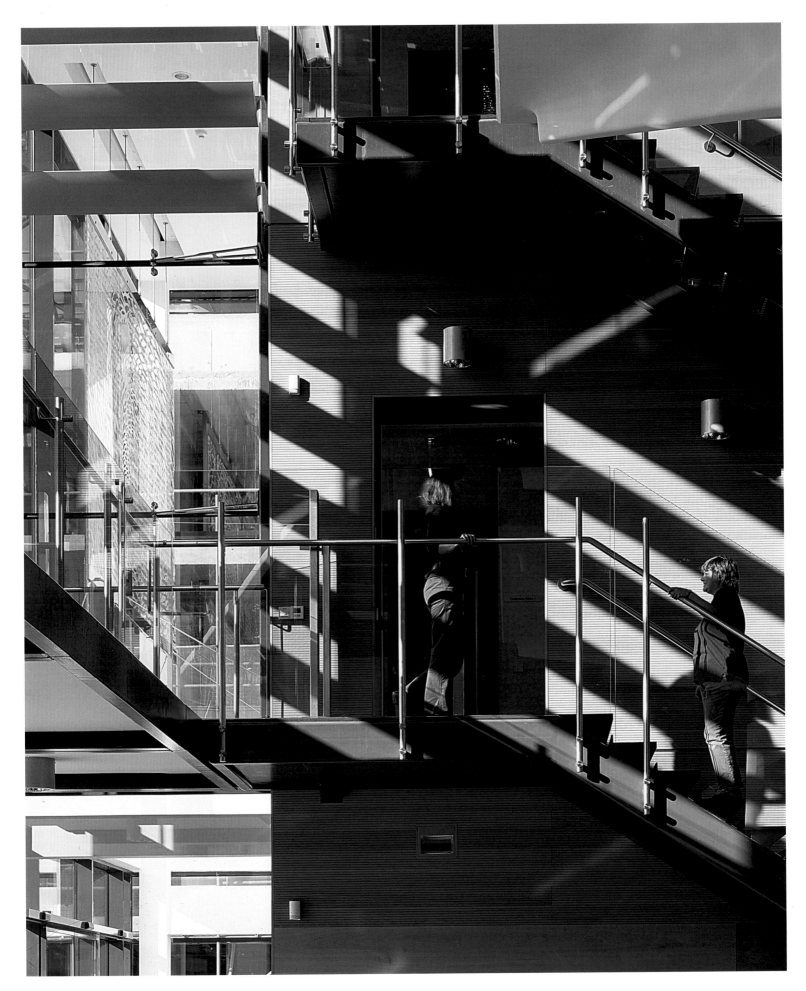

LEWIS GLUCKSMAN GALLERY
.CORK .IRELAND
.O'DONNELL + TUOMEY

The Lewis Glucksman Gallery has a civic role in addressing University College Cork and the city beyond. It also has a picturesque role in settling into an important mature landscape. That the building handles this difficult tension with ease is a mark of the incredible skill that the architects have brought to it.

In a way the architecture is full of contradictions: it uses such everyday materials as galvanized steel and MDF, yet it manages to appear luxurious (but not decadent); it has a truly astonishing cantilever, but it feels as if it should be there (rather than being a gestural shout); the walls of the gallery, which by tradition should be orthogonal, have bends in them, and they work; the building occupies the tight footprint of two previous tennis courts but inside has a Tardis-like quality through the continuity of route and space; it employs none of the classical tropes for beauty but looks astonishingly good; the galleries have a feeling of concentrated internality, and yet one is always connected to the outside; the detailing is under complete control but never fetishized. This is a rich and intellectually stimulating building.

To understand the experience one follows a *promenade architecturale*. This starts with one of the main routes of the university that cuts straight beneath the underbelly of the galleries above. Le Corbusier used a similar trick, driving a major pedestrian route through the Carpenter Center at Harvard, but there the effect is to turn the visitors into voyeurs; at Cork it democratically opens up the building to anyone. From the entrance one either descends (guided by cold steel handrail) into the stone-clad, earthbound lower floors seemingly cut from the raw landscape, or rises (guided by warm timber) to the galleries above. Here one is nudged but not cajoled on a route upwards until, at the top, just when one thinks one has reached a cul-de-sac and will have to retrace one's steps, a small staircase releases the tension and spins one back down. Along the route are incidents and placements that are beautifully judged, adding variety without being invasive.

What is really remarkable about this building is that the more one looks, the better it gets. That is the sign of complete assurance and maturity. This building belongs to the canon of modern buildings. Miles Davis once said that what most artists do is to make simple things complex, but what great artists (and of course that included him) do is to make complex things appear simple. This is one of those rare buildings that fits that definition of greatness.

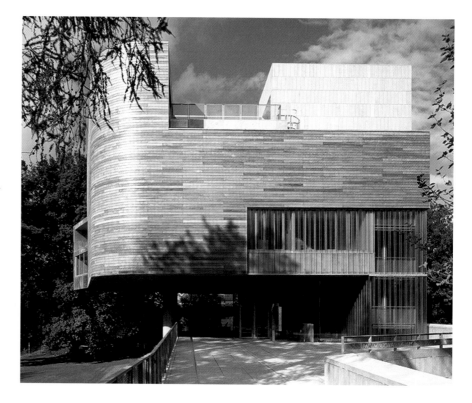

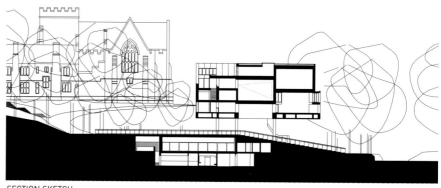

SECTION SKETCH

ABOVE O'Donnell + Tuomey's sketches give a good idea of the sylvan campus context and deserve to be hung on the gallery walls.

TOP AND OPPOSITE The architects have cut a public route through the gallery, directly beneath the dramatic cantilevers, tempting passers-by into its rich interiors.

CLIENT University College Cork **STRUCTURAL ENGINEER** Horgan Lynch & Partners **CONTRACTOR** P.J. Hegarty & Sons **CONTRACT VALUE** £7 million **PHOTOGRAPHER** Dennis Gilbert – VIEW

McLAREN TECHNOLOGY CENTRE
.WOKING, SURREY .FOSTER AND PARTNERS

One arrives at the McLaren building having travelled around the lake, in Norman Foster's words, "as if driving up to a country house". The experience is perhaps more akin to Arthur C. Clarke than Agatha Christie. At first concealed by large undulating grass mounds, the curved glazed façade suddenly appears in view, standing alone except for its own reflection in the lake. It is a building that symbolizes McLaren, constructed with great precision in a meeting of minds, the client and architect sharing the same aspirations.

This new headquarters building also accommodates studios, laboratories, research testing facilities, electronic development, machine shops, prototyping and production facilities for McLaren's Formula One cars and the Mercedes-Benz SLR McLaren.

The symbiotic relationship that exists between architect and client is mirrored by that between McLaren and its suppliers, whether they be Schüco, which developed the glass façade with McLaren; Boss, which supplies the black T-shirts and jeans worn by all the staff; or TAG Heuer, which keeps the time at the factory and on the track. All McLaren's partners not only benefit from having an award-winning building to showcase their work; they are also expected to contribute to and share in the success of the Formula One team.

The plan of the main building is roughly semicircular, the circle being completed by a newly created formal lake, an integral part of the building's cooling system. Reed beds are also used to manage surface-water drainage as part of the environmental strategy. The principal lakeside façade is a continuous curved glass wall, shaded by a cantilevered roof. Internally there is one main double-height street, 200 metres long, where classic sports and racing cars are lined up like trophies in a glass cabinet (the trophies themselves are round the corner). The main street defines circulation and articulates the fingers of accommodation, which are separated by other 6-metre-wide streets. On the ground floor are the production and storage areas, as well as the hospitality suites and a staff restaurant, which look out across the lake. Top-lit studios, offices and meeting rooms are at first-floor level. A basement accommodates technical areas, including a wind tunnel.

The build quality is remarkable, with exemplary detailing. This is a mature and confident scheme, six years in the making. Every detail has been considered, from the structural glazing to bolt heads and artwork. Many areas are breathtaking, and even the more soulless parts are enlivened by colourful glass art installations.

David Nelson, the partner in charge of the project at Foster and Partners and an industrial designer by training, rather than an architect, was impressed by the client's attention to detail: "It's a kind of thinking you don't normally get in architecture. McLaren's standards are so high. Compared to the manufacturing industry at this level, the construction industry is miles behind, and very crude in comparison."

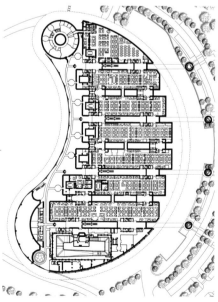

ABOVE AND OPPOSITE TOP The kidney-bean plan of the building is complemented by the lake, which acts as a flattering mirror and an essential part of the centre's cooling and drainage systems.

OPPOSITE BOTTOM The main double-height street links all the production areas and acts as a starting grid for the company's former stars.

CLIENT McLaren Group **STRUCTURAL ENGINEER** Arup **CONTRACTOR** Kier Build
CONTRACT VALUE Confidential **PHOTOGRAPHERS** Paul Grundy – McLaren Group (above)/
Nigel Young – Foster and Partners (opposite)

FIRST-FLOOR PLAN

THE STIRLING PRIZE 2005
.DEYAN SUDJIC
ARCHITECTURE CRITIC OF *THE OBSERVER*

On the face of it, the quality of the tenth shortlist for the Stirling Prize suggested that contemporary architecture in Britain is in rude good health. In some years the selection could fairly have been described as the bland leading the bland. Not in 2005; the judges had the pick of everything from Zaha Hadid's most powerfully sculptural work to date, in the shape of her new factory for BMW at Leipzig, a project in which she managed to combine her spatial vision with an engagement in the life of the production line; by way of Foster and Partners' undulating glass ribbon headquarters building for the McLaren racing team; to the enormously inventive, and equally enormously costly, Scottish Parliament. In this company, O'Donnell + Tuomey's Glucksman Gallery in Cork was, for a while, a somewhat unlikely bookies' favourite, but the gallery would certainly have been a worthwhile winner. So would Hadid's project. But despite the impressive quality of the finalists, there is still something not quite right about Britain's most valuable architecture prize, not least because choosing between a work as elegantly modest as O'Donnell + Tuomey's gallery and a building as sweepingly operatic as the Scottish Parliament is impossible. The parliament is a building that will still be talked about in a hundred years' time. It's already part of a landscape, imprinted on the national mindset. It stands as a reproach to those architects who believe that architecture can be reduced to a skin, a managerial process or a collection of fashionable mannerisms.

Beyond the difficulty of choosing between this year's nominees, something about the prize that aspires to do for buildings what the Man Booker does for books, and the Turner does for art, fails to add up. The real problem faced by the Stirling Prize since its launch in 1996 has been its failure to come up with a coherent sense of what the award is for, and then to stick with it. If the point of setting up the £20,000 award that carries his name really was to honour the memory of James Stirling, one of Britain's greatest post-war architects, as is sometimes suggested, so far it has not been much of a success. Since Stirling's premature death in 1992, the whimsical games he played with architectural history have become deeply unfashionable. For the time being at least, Stirling's work is trapped in a critical deep freeze.

Despite the rhetoric, however, celebrating James Stirling's architectural achievements was no more the point of the award than celebrating the man who painted *The Fighting Temeraire* was of the Tate's Turner Prize. In fact, what the RIBA seems to be trying to do is to make the world think about architects more warmly. The ceremony is certainly a much glossier affair than it was even five years ago, when Will Alsop, warmed by the generosity of the sponsor's champagne, did a Tracey Emin and gave a national audience the rough end of his tongue while waiting to collect the prize for his library in Peckham.

The effect of the prize on the public perception of contemporary British architecture is less clear. It's hard convincingly to equate the course of architectural history in the past ten years with the Stirling Prize winners to date. Some, undoubtedly, are definitive works: you couldn't tell the story of world architecture, still less British architecture, without including the 2004 winner, Norman Foster's 30 St Mary Axe, which served to redefine the form of the office tower. But the award has had its curious blind spots too. In some years it seems to have missed the point altogether.

It is puzzling, for example, that Piers Gough, one of the jurors in 2005, has not collected the prize himself. And David Chipperfield is certainly one of Britain's best-regarded architects internationally, responsible for a range of museums across Europe and America. But he has never won the award either. Can the list really reflect the best that architecture in Britain has to offer, particularly in this exceptionally busy time? Who now would seriously suggest that Wilkinson Eyre's winning Magna Centre, carved from a redundant steelworks, the charms of which lay largely in its raw state before the architects arrived, is a great work? Certainly the prize has proved vital for several of the winners. Future Systems collected the £20,000 cheque in 1999 for the NatWest Media Centre at Lord's. It marked the practice's first major commission, and without the prize money it could well have been its last. The practice's bank manager was on the verge of calling in its overdraft before the ceremony.

The most serious charge against the prize is that it has tended to reward the inoffensive rather than promote a strong idea of what British architecture should be. The shortlist in 2005 tells us less about the nature of architecture than it does about the peculiarities of the way that we approach the subject. It demonstrates, for example, that Germany is more likely to hire Zaha Hadid than is Britain, that the provision of civic buildings in the United Kingdom has been privatized for no obvious reason, and that if you want to find lyrical but rational architecture you have to look at Ireland.

A prize that could counter some of these disappointing tendencies would be worth having. A prize that looked at work that reflects some of the qualities that made James Stirling's work so interesting would be a good start. Awarding the prize to O'Donnell + Tuomey would have been a useful first step in that direction. Certainly, there would be a certain symmetry involved. The pair worked for James Stirling in the late 1970s and the 1980s, and their work clearly draws on some of his ideas about rooting architecture in precedent and context. These are issues that are hardly discussed in a serious way today. Memory, it seems, is off the architectural agenda. Perhaps it is time to bring it back. It would be encouraging to think that an award could be used to convey a more complex message than the triumph of spectacle, and that an architectural prize can still be about more than the egotistical object or a reward for corporate good manners.

THE STIRLING PRIZE: THE ONES THAT GOT AWAY

.HUGH PEARMAN

So there I am, sitting at the Grimshaw table in the Great Court of the British Museum for the Stirling Prize ceremony of 2001. The whole team is there, and so is Tim Smit, the client for the Eden Project in Cornwall. This is the fancied project. This is the clear favourite. After all the televisual preliminaries, it's announcement time. And the winner is ... hang on, why aren't the cameras pointing at us? ... the Magna Centre in Rotherham by Wilkinson Eyre.

Whaaaat? Smit's expression turns thunderous. Nick Grimshaw's is impassive. Andrew Whalley, Grimshaw's director in charge of Eden, gives a rueful smile. As the applause dies down, Whalley leans over to me. "Oh well," he mutters, "at least we've got the Hot-dip Galvanizing Award." Such humour in the face of cruel fate deserves its own award, and gets it a few minutes later when Chris Wilkinson, ever the gentleman, comes over to shake Grimshaw's hand. "You should have won it", he says. He's not the only one in the hall saying that. This was the first year of the judges' secret ballot.

Suddenly everything goes wobbly and I'm back a few years earlier, 1998, in the shoestring-budget, pre-television, pre-PowerPoint days of the prize, when we are all jammed into the RIBA's Florence Hall on long tables equipped with Jenga, out of which we are making competing buildings. The Jenga is a huge success after a few glasses of wine. But I'm not having a lot of fun. The trouble is, I'm sitting next to Rick Mather. He's great company, but I have a ghastly secret. I'm one of the judges. I know he hasn't won. I also know how close the decision was. Indeed, I know that he had damn near won it at one stage for a wonderful house he built in Hampstead. But at the last minute (in fact, overnight) our acting chairman changed his mind. That meant that the winner would not be Mather after all, but Norman Foster for his American Air Museum at Duxford.

There was a bit of a *brouhaha* about that. The president, David Rock, who had missed the vote through illness, was visited on his sickbed to adjudicate, and the decision stood. So on the night, there I am next to Mather when Foster (who is absent) wins it. Not that the urbane Mather would ever show disappointment. It's the Stirling Prize jinx: no one-off house by any architect has yet won it. No reason in principle why not, but in practice houses are soaked up by the ancillary awards. One day, perhaps.

Maybe Duxford was a worthier winner, as a public building. Looking back, few people now remember the Mather house. It's private, tucked away: few people go there or are even aware of its existence. In contrast, everyone knows about Eden, whereas rather fewer know its nemesis, Magna. Eden struck a public chord in a way that Wilkinson Eyre's converted steelworks of a science centre, for all its ingenuity and success as a destination, did not.

But at least Magna carries a torch for the imaginative conversion project. Tate Modern – a conversion of a power station – did not win the Stirling Prize, although that was all to do with Byzantine RIBA rules about overseas architects. It couldn't be entered, so Herzog & de Meuron was the ghost at the feast in 2001. Later, this anomaly was sorted. Tate Modern's architects won the prize in 2003 for their Laban dance centre in London's Deptford.

It wasn't just the big gallery on Bankside. London certainly lost out, awards-wise, with its Millennium crop of buildings. Neither the Royal Opera House nor the National Portrait Gallery Ondaatje Wing, both by Dixon.Jones, reached the top of the Stirling ladder. Nor did Richard MacCormac's Wellcome Wing at the Science Museum, or Foster and Partners' Great Court at the British Museum. Given that the prize ceremony had been held in both these venues in previous years, perhaps everyone had got a bit tired of them. Tip: don't let your building go stale. Enter it as early as you decently can. Judges like fresh architecture. Familiarity breeds contempt.

Mind you, around the time of the Millennium it was understandable that architects should have agonized over when to enter their buildings. There were so many to choose from. How extraordinary, for instance, that Michael Wilford's Lowry in Salford should have got no further than the basic RIBA Award in 2001. I'd have expected it to get on to the shortlist rather than Magna. But here's the second problem: what if you've got more than one eligible building? Wilford did, and that year it was his British Embassy in Berlin that found itself elevated to the shortlist, though no further.

It happens every time. Every shortlist has at least one candidate on it that at least one of the judges will be convinced is rubbish compared with some other scheme that inexplicably didn't make the cut. And then, when it comes to the announcement of the winner, people will throw up their hands in disbelief that Building A won the prize rather than Building B or Building C. It's part of the fun of the thing, but it also highlights the sudden-death aspects of such awards. Even the judges – *especially* the judges, and I speak with feeling – can be astonished by the outcome. And let's not forget that there is more than glory at stake here. There's the little matter of £20,000. People badly want to win, and there can be real anger and frustration when they don't.

Right back at the start of all this, in the first year of the prize in 1996, I was slightly puzzled that a rather good rural factory in Northamptonshire hadn't got further than the first round. That was the Doc Martens shoe factory outside Wellingborough, and it was by the then very young practice of Haworth Tompkins. It was a nice exercise in modern vernacular; at a casual glance you might think it was a better class of farm building, but when you went to see it you found a highly sophisticated sequence of spaces. Graham Haworth and Steve Tompkins later hit the big time with their radical rebuild of the Royal Court Theatre for Stephen Daldry, and are now doing the Young Vic and the London Library. Should the regional jury have spotted the early potential? Come to that, should the judges have been kinder on the maverick buildings knocking around that year, such as John Outram's joyously polychromatic Judge Institute in Cambridge or Short Ford's positively baroque Queens Building at De Montfort University in Leicester, a pioneer in low-energy, naturally ventilated architecture on a civic scale?

What this kind of thing tells us is that – in those slightly shambolic early days at any rate, and for all I know it may still be true today – the whole RIBA awards process runs the risk of being over-judged. It's the principled opposite of those lesser awards that are declared on the basis of a few photos, but with so many filters before the Stirling shortlist, there is always the danger that more *outré* contenders may lose out to the safer mainstream. The more tiers there are, the more the opportunities for sudden death. Thus we mourn for the Tintin space-fungus of Future Systems' Birmingham Selfridges, which deserved a better run for sheer chutzpah.

But enough of all that. As we've seen, most years there is enough controversy to be found among the handful of buildings that comprise the Stirling shortlist itself. Take the second year, 1997. The headline then was that the Stirling Prize had been won by a Stirling building. And indeed, the Music School at Stuttgart was a Stirling Wilford product, albeit one that had been brought to fruition by Michael Wilford in the years following Jim's death. But the point was that everyone expected this to be Will Alsop's year. His breakthrough, competition-winning building with John Lyall, his emergence on to the international stage, was with the regional government headquarters in Marseilles, better known as Le Grand Bleu, or the 'Big Blue'. This, for the first time, was an Alsop manifesto building achieved on a large scale. Interesting that the judges' choice should have been between two utterly different kinds of Post-modern buildings, although the creators of both will presumably reject that tag.

In those days, the final decision was made by consensus rather than through a secret vote. Persuasive arguments by the judges perhaps counted more. One of the judges that year in particular was entranced by the sheer build quality of the Stirling/Wilford building. The Music School certainly contrasted with the slightly flaky feel of the Big Blue, which, at the time of our visit, did not appear to be wearing well in the Mediterranean sun. Still, it would have been a very popular winner. Alsop was understandably miffed. But talent will out, and he won in 2000 for his Peckham Library, when most people expected the prize to go to another building, of course. And that one was ...

The New Art Gallery Walsall by Caruso St John. Much as I love Alsop and the Peckham Library, much as I applauded his famously profane acceptance speech, I wish, how I wish, that Walsall had won the Stirling. I went back there recently to see how it is getting on, and it is looking better all the time – calm, dignified, slightly alien, every detail perfectly executed, sumptuously austere and now, at last, starting to generate new developments around it. Only with the Lottery largesse around the Millennium could such a building in such a place have been built by such a young and relatively untried firm of architects. This is the antidote to all those media reports of Lottery projects going wrong and closing down. It is just triumphantly good, and it is giving the post-industrial town of Walsall hope.

Other years have flung up other quirks. The first Stirling Prize I really enjoyed was the first one I wasn't involved in, and the first to be held outside London. It was 1999, in Glasgow, and I didn't have to do anything other than turn up at the Kelvingrove Art Gallery and cheer as Jan Kaplicky and Amanda Levete of Future Systems won for their NatWest Media Centre. However, there was a chill undercurrent that year that had swept in from Edinburgh. It was called the Museum of Scotland, by Benson + Forsyth. And at first it hadn't been shortlisted.

It was that old regional juries problem. It was also the unfashionable architecture problem. Although the Museum of Scotland is very different from Colin St John Wilson's British Library at St Pancras, for instance, both buildings are astonishingly dedicated total works of art, every detail being considered by their architects. They are heavyweight, masonry buildings in the monumental tradition. The British Library had to be magicked on to the shortlist in 1998 against a fair bit of opposition. The same had to be done for the Museum of Scotland in 1999. It was absurd that nationally important civic buildings of such quality should be overlooked simply because they were somewhat out of step with the fashions of the time. Of course, neither won, but time is on their side.

So it continues. Why, oh why did Ted Cullinan's masterly Downland Gridshell get pipped by Wilkinson Eyre's Gateshead Millennium Bridge in 2002? Well, I can see why: it's a marvel of a bridge, and I don't agree with those who say it's not a building. That's the merciless pity of the process: there has to be one winner out of a shortlist that, in a good year, might have two or three real contenders. There's such potential for conflict. It's good television, though.

So here's to all those buildings that should or could have won, or ought at any rate to have been contenders but – as a result of mysterious and possibly sinister forces or just a curious kind of entropy in the foothills of the process – did not. Nobody will ever fully agree. It's a topic that gets everyone animated every time architecture buffs gather together. It's like soccer fans reliving the clincher goal that was unfairly disallowed. Did someone collar the referee at half-time? (No, ed.)

INDEX

ACKNOWLEDGEMENTS

I would like to thank all the judges of the Stirling Prize and the RIBA Awards, who gave up so much time to choose the winners and whose original citations form the basis of parts of this book.

I would also like to thank the ten independent journalists who were commissioned by the RIBA to express their personal views on the ten shortlists. Needless to say, their views do not always represent those of the RIBA, otherwise history would be very different.

Especial thanks are due to the three sponsors of the RIBA Stirling Prize over its ten years: *The Sunday Times*, *RIBA Journal* and *The Architects' Journal*. Their generosity has made a number of architects very happy, and their editorial support has helped the prize to grow.

Finally, I would particularly like to thank Nancy Mills, Sue Woods and Caz Facey, who have run the RIBA Awards throughout the Stirling era. Their unfailing good humour and efficiency in coping with an ever-expanding number of entrants and an increasingly high-profile prize have made Stirling what it is today.